Carter Godwin Woodson (December 19, 1875 – April 3, 1950) was an American historian, author, journalist, and the founder of the Association for the Study of African American Life and History. He was one of the first scholars to study the history of the African diaspora, including African-American history. A founder of The Journal of Negro History in 1916, Woodson has been called the "father of black history".In February 1926 he launched the celebration of "Negro History Week", the precursor of Black History Month.

CARTER G. WOODSON

A CENTURY OF NEGRO MIGRATION

A CENTURY OF NEGRO MIGRATION
by CARTER G. WOODSON

Edition copyright © Delhi Open Books, 2021

Published by

Delhi Open Books

G/F, 4771/23, Bharat Ram Road, Daryaganj, New Delhi-110002
Ph.: 91-11-42408081
E-mail: **delhiopenbooks2016@gmail.com**

ISBN: 978-93-92355-07-3

Cover, Typesetting, and Book Design by **ROHIT**

Contents

CHAPTER 1. FINDING A PLACE OF REFUGE

The migration of the blacks from the Southern States to those offering them better opportunities is nothing new. The objective here, therefore, will be not merely to present the causes and results of the recent movement of the Negroes to the North but to connect this event with the periodical movements of the blacks to that section, from about the year 1815 to the present day. That this movement should date from that period indicates that the policy of the commonwealths towards the Negro must have then begun decidedly to differ so as to make one section of the country more congenial to the despised blacks than the other. As a matter of fact, to justify this conclusion, we need but give passing mention here to developments too well known to be discussed in detail. Slavery in the original thirteen States was the normal condition of the Negroes. When, however, James Otis, Patrick Henry and Thomas Jefferson began to discuss the natural rights of the colonists, then said to be oppressed by Great Britain, some of the patriots of the Revolution carried their reasoning to its logical conclusion, contending that the Negro slaves should be freed on the same grounds, as their rights were also founded in the laws of nature. And so it was soon done in most Northern commonwealths.

Vermont, New Hampshire, and Massachusetts exterminated the institution by constitutional provision and Rhode Island, Connecticut, New Jersey, New York and Pennsylvania by gradual emancipation acts. And it was thought that the institution would soon thereafter pass away even in all southern commonwealths except South Carolina and Georgia, where it had seemingly become profitable. There came later the industrial revolution following the invention of Watt's steam engine and mechanical appliances like Whitney's cotton gin, all which changed the economic aspect of the modern world, making slavery an institution offering means of exploitation to those engaged in the production of cotton. This revolution rendered necessary a large supply of cheap labor for cotton culture, out of which the plantation system grew. The Negro slaves, therefore, lost all hope of ever winning their freedom in South Carolina and Georgia; and in Maryland, Virginia, and North

Carolina, where the sentiment in favor of abolition had been favorable, there was a decided reaction which soon blighted their hopes. In the Northern commonwealths, however, the sentiment in behalf of universal freedom, though at times dormant, was ever apparent despite the attachment to the South of the trading classes of northern cities, which profited by the slave trade and their commerce with the slaveholding States. The Northern States maintaining this liberal attitude developed, therefore, into an asylum for the Negroes who were oppressed in the South.

The Negroes, however, were not generally welcomed in the North. Many of the northerners who sympathized with the oppressed blacks in the South never dreamt of having them as their neighbors. There were, consequently, always two classes of anti-slavery people, those who advocated the abolition of slavery to elevate the blacks to the dignity of citizenship, and those who merely hoped to exterminate the institution because it was an economic evil. The latter generally believed that the blacks constituted an inferior class that could not discharge the duties of citizenship, and when the proposal to incorporate the blacks into the body politic was clearly presented to these agitators their anti-slavery ardor was decidedly dampened. Unwilling, however, to take the position that a race should be doomed because of personal objections, many of the early anti-slavery group looked toward colonization for a solution of this problem. Some thought of Africa, but since the deportation of a large number of persons who had been brought under the influence of modern civilization seemed cruel, the most popular colonization scheme at first seemed to be that of settling the Negroes on the public lands in the West. As this region had been lately ceded, however, and no one could determine what use could be made of it by white men, no such policy was generally accepted.

When this territory was ceded to the United States an effort to provide for the government of it finally culminated in the proposed Ordinance of 1784 carrying the provision that slavery should not exist in the Northwest Territory after the year 1800. This measure finally failed to pass and fortunately too, thought some, because, had slavery been given sixteen years of growth on that soil, it might not have been abolished there until the Civil War or it might have caused such a preponderance of slave commonwealths as to make the rebellion successful. The Ordinance of 1784 was antecedent to the more important Ordinance of 1787, which carried the famous sixth article that neither slavery nor involuntary servitude except as a punishment for crime should exist in that territory. At first, it was generally deemed feasible to establish Negro colonies on that domain. Yet despite the assurance of the Ordinance of 1787 conditions were such that one could not determine exactly whether the Northwest Territory would be slave or free.

What then was the situation in this partly unoccupied territory? Slavery existed in what is now the Northwest Territory from the time of the early exploration and settlement of that region by the French. The first slaves of white men were Indians. Though it is true that the red men usually chose death rather than slavery, there were some of them that bowed to the yoke. So many Pawnee Indians became bondsmen that the word Pani became synonymous with slave in the West. Western Indians themselves, following the custom of white men, enslaved their captives in war rather than choose the alternative of putting them to death. In this way they were known to hold a number of blacks and whites.

The enslavement of the black man by the whites in this section dates from the early part of the eighteenth century. Being a part of the Louisiana Territory which under France extended over the whole Mississippi Valley as far as the Allegheny mountains, it was governed by the same colonial regulations. Slavery, therefore, had legal standing in this territory. When Antoine Crozat, upon being placed in control of Louisiana, was authorized to begin a traffic in slaves, Crozat himself did nothing to carry out his plan. But in 1717 when the control of the colony was transferred to the Compagnie de l'Occident steps were taken toward the importation of slaves. In 1719, when 500 Guinea Negroes were brought over to serve in Lower Louisiana, Philip Francis Renault imported 500 other bondsmen into Upper Louisiana or what was later included in the Northwest Territory. Slavery then became more and more extensive until by 1750 there were along the Mississippi five settlements of slaves, Kaskaskia, Kaokia, Fort Chartres, St. Phillipe and Prairie du Rocher. In 1763 Negroes were relatively numerous in the Northwest Territory but when this section that year was transferred to the British the number was diminished by the action of those Frenchmen who, unwilling to become subjects of Great Britain, moved from the territory. There was no material increase in the slave population thereafter until the end of the eighteenth century when some Negroes came from the original thirteen.

The Ordinance of 1787 did not disturb the relation of slave and master. Some pioneers thought that the sixth article exterminated slavery there; others contended that it did not.

The latter believed that such expressions in the Ordinance of 1787 as the "free inhabitants" and the "free male inhabitants of full size" implied the continuance of slavery and others found ground for its perpetuation in that clause of the Ordinance which allowed the people of the territory to adopt the constitution and laws of any one of the thirteen States. Students of law saw protection for slavery in Jay's treaty which guaranteed to the settlers their property of all kinds. When, therefore, the slave question came up in the Northwest Territory about the close of the eighteenth century, there were three classes of slaves: first, those who were in servitude to French owners previous to the cession of the Territory to England and were still claimed as property in the possession of which the owners were protected under the treaty of 1763; second, those who were held by British owners at the time of Jay's treaty and claimed afterward as property under its protection; and third, those who, since the Territory had been controlled by the United States, had been brought from the commonwealths in which slavery was allowed. Freedom, however, was recognized as the ultimate status of the Negro in that territory.

This question having been seemingly settled, Anthony Benezet, who for years advocated the abolition of slavery and devoted his time and means to the preparation of the Negroes for living as freedmen, was practical enough to recommend to the Congress of the Confederation a plan of colonizing the emancipated blacks on the western lands. Jefferson incorporated into his scheme for a modern system of public schools the training of the slaves in industrial and agricultural branches to equip them for a higher station in life. He believed, however, that the blacks not being equal to the white race should not be assimilated and should they be free, they should, by all means, be colonized afar off. Thinking that the western lands might be so used, he said in writing to James Monroe in

1801: "A very great extent of country north of the Ohio has been laid off in townships, and is now at market, according to the provisions of the act of Congress…. There is nothing," said he, "which would restrain the State of Virginia either in the purchase or the application of these lands." Yet he raised the question as to whether the establishment of such a colony within our limits and to become a part of the Union would be desirable. He thought then of procuring a place beyond the limits of the United States on our northern boundary, by purchasing the Indian lands with the consent of Great Britain. He then doubted that the black race would live in such a rigorous climate.

This plan did not easily pass from the minds of the friends of the slaves, for in 1805 Thomas Brannagan asserted in his Serious Remonstrances that the government should appropriate a few thousand acres of land at some distant part of the national domains for the Negroes' accommodation and support. He believed that the new State might be established upwards of 2,000 miles from our frontier. A copy of the pamphlet containing this proposition was sent to Thomas Jefferson, who was impressed thereby, but not having the courage to brave the torture of being branded as a friend of the slave, he failed to give it his support. The same question was brought prominently before the public again in 1816 when there was presented to the House of Representatives a memorial from the Kentucky Abolition Society praying that the free people of color be colonized on the public lands. The committee to whom the memorial was referred for consideration reported that it was expedient to refuse the request on the ground that, as such lands were not granted to free white men, they saw no reason for granting them to others.

Some Negro slaves unwilling to wait to be carried or invited to the Northwest Territory escaped to that section even when it was controlled by the French prior to the American

Revolution. Slaves who reached the West by this route caused trouble between the French and the British colonists.

Advertising in 1746 for James Wenyam, a slave, Richard Colgate, his master, said that he swore to a Negro whom he endeavored to induce to go with him, that he had often been in the backwoods with his master and that he would go to the French and Indians and fight for them. In an advertisement for a mulatto slave in 1755 Thomas Ringold, his master, expressed fear that he had escaped by the same route to the French. He, therefore, said: "It seems to be the interest, at least, of every gentleman that has slaves, to be active in the beginning of these attempts, for whilst we have the French such near neighbors, we shall not have the least security in that kind of property."

The good treatment which these slaves received among the French, and especially at Pittsburgh the gateway to the Northwest Territory, tended to make that city an asylum for those slaves who had sufficient spirit of adventure to brave the wilderness through which they had to go. Negroes even then had the idea that there was in this country a place of more privilege than those they enjoyed in the seaboard colonies. Knowing of the likelihood of the Negroes to rise during the French and Indian War, Governor Dinwiddie wrote Fox one of the Secretaries of State in 1756: "We dare not venture to part with any of our white men any distance, as we must have a watchful eye over our Negro slaves, who are upward of one hundred thousand." Brissot de Warville mentions in his Travels of 1788 several examples of marriages of white and blacks in Pittsburgh. He noted the case of a Negro who married an indentured French servant woman. Out of this union came a desirable mulatto girl who married a surgeon of Nantes then stationed at Pittsburgh. His family was considered one of the most respectable of the city. The Negro referred to was doing a creditable business and his wife took it upon herself to welcome foreigners, especially the French, who came that way. Along the Ohio also there were several cases of women of color living with unmarried white men; but this was looked upon by the Negroes as detestable as was evidenced by the fact that, if black women had a quarrel with a mulatto woman, the former would reproach the latter for being of ignoble blood.

These tendencies, however, could not assure the Negro that the Northwest Territory was to be an asylum for freedom when in 1763 it passed into the hands of the British, the promoters of the slave trade, and later to the independent colonies, two of which had no desire to exterminate slavery.

Furthermore, when the Ordinance of 1787 with its famous sixth article against slavery was proclaimed, it was soon discovered that this document was not necessarily emancipatory. As the right to hold slaves was guaranteed to those who owned them prior to the passage of the Ordinance of 1787, it was to be expected that those attached to that institution would not indifferently see it pass away. Various petitions, therefore, were sent to the territorial legislature and to Congress praying that the sixth article of the Ordinance of 1787 be abrogated. No formal action to this effect was taken, but the practice of slavery was continued even at the winking of the government. Some slaves came from the Canadians who, in accordance with the slave trade laws of the British Empire, were supplied with bondsmen. It was the Canadians themselves who provided by act of parliament in 1793 for prohibiting the importation of slaves and for gradual emancipation. When it seemed later that the cause of freedom would eventually triumph the proslavery element undertook to perpetuate slavery through a system of indentured servant labor.

In the formation of the States of Indiana and Illinois the question as to what should be done to harmonize with the new constitution the system of indenture to which the territorial legislatures had been committed, caused heated debate and at times almost conflict. Both Indiana and Illinois finally incorporated into their constitutions compromise provisions for a nominal prohibition of slavery modified by clauses for the continuation of the system of indentured labor of the Negroes held to service. The proslavery party persistently struggled for some years to secure by the interpretation of the laws, by legislation and even by amending the constitution so to change the fundamental law as to provide for actual slavery. These States, however, gradually worked toward freedom in keeping with the spirit of the majority who framed the constitution, despite the fact that the indenture system in southern Illinois and especially in Indiana was at times tantamount to slavery as it was practiced in parts of the South.

It must be borne in mind here, however, that the North at this time was far from becoming a place of refuge for Negroes. In the first place, the industrial revolution had not then had time to reduce the Negroes to the plane of beasts in the cotton kingdom. The rigorous climate and the industries of the northern people, moreover, were not inviting to the blacks and the development of the carrying trade and the rise of manufacturing there did not make that section more attractive to unskilled labor.

Furthermore, when we consider the fact that there were many thousands of Negroes in the Southern States the presence of a few in the North must be regarded as insignificant. This paucity of blacks then obtained especially in the Northwest Territory, for its French inhabitants instead of being an exploiting people were pioneering, having little use for slaves in carrying out their policy of merely holding the country for France. Moreover, like certain gentlemen from Virginia, who after the American Revolution were afraid to bring their slaves with them to occupy their bounty lands in Ohio, few enterprising settlers from the slave States had invaded the territory with their Negroes, not knowing whether or not they would be secure in the possession of such property. When we consider that in 1810 there were only 102,137 Negroes in the North and no more than 3,454 in the Northwest Territory, we must look to the second decade of the nineteenth century for the beginning of the migration of the Negroes in the United States.

CHAPTER 2. A TRANSPLANTATION TO THE NORTH

Just after the settlement of the question of holding the western posts by the British and the adjustment of the trouble arising from their capture of slaves during our second war with England, there started a movement of the blacks to this frontier territory. But, as there were few towns or cities in the Northwest during the first decades of the new republic, the flight of the Negro into that territory was like that of a fugitive taking his chances in the wilderness. Having lost their pioneering spirit in passing through the ordeal of slavery, not many of the bondmen took flight in that direction and few free Negroes ventured to seek their fortunes in those wilds during the period of the frontier conditions, especially when the country had not then undergone a thorough reaction against the Negro.

The migration of the Negroes, however, received an impetus early in the nineteenth century. This came from the Quakers, who by the middle of the eighteenth century had taken the position that all members of their sect should free their slaves. The Quakers of North Carolina and Virginia had as early as 1740 taken up the serious question of humanely treating their Negroes. The North Carolina Quakers advised Friends to emancipate their slaves, later prohibited traffic in them, forbade their members from even hiring the blacks out in 1780 and by 1818 had exterminated the institution among their communicants. After healing themselves of the sin, they had before the close of the eighteenth century militantly addressed themselves to the task of abolishing slavery and the slave trade throughout the world. Differing in their scheme from that of most anti-slavery leaders, they were advocating the establishment of the freedmen in society as good citizens and to that end had provided for the religious and mental instruction of their slaves prior to emancipating them.

Despite the fact that the Quakers were not free to extend their operations throughout the colonies, they did much to enable the Negroes to reach free soil. As the Quakers believed in the freedom of the will, human brotherhood, and equality before God, they did not, like the Puritans, find difficulties in solving the problem of elevating the Negroes. Whereas certain Puritans were afraid that conversion might lead to the destruction of caste and the incorporation of undesirable persons into the "Body Politick," the Quakers proceeded on the principle that all men are brethren and, being equal before God, should be considered equal before the law. On account of unduly emphasizing the relation of man to God, the Puritans "atrophied their social humanitarian instinct" and developed into a race of self- conscious saints. Believing in human nature and laying stress upon the relation between man and man, the Quakers became the friends of all humanity.

In 1693 George Keith, a leading Quaker of his day, came forward as a promoter of the religious training of the slaves as a preparation for emancipation. William Penn advocated the emancipation of slaves, that they might have every opportunity for improvement. In 1695 the Quakers while protesting against the slave trade denounced also the policy of neglecting their moral and spiritual welfare. The growing interest of this sect in the Negroes was shown later by the development in 1713 of a definite scheme for freeing and returning them to Africa after having been educated and trained to serve as missionaries on that continent.

When the manumission of the slaves was checked by the reaction against that class and it became more of a problem to establish them in a hostile environment, certain Quakers of

North Carolina and Virginia adopted the scheme of settling them in Northern States. At first, they sent such freedmen to Pennsylvania. But for various reasons this did not prove to be the best asylum. In the first place, Pennsylvania bordered on the slave States, Maryland and Virginia, from which agents came to kidnap free Negroes. Furthermore, too many Negroes were already rushing to that commonwealth as the Negroes' heaven and there was the chance that the Negroes might be settled elsewhere in the North, where they might have better economic opportunities. A committee of forty was accordingly appointed by North Carolina Quakers in 1822 to examine the laws of other free States with a view to determining what section would be most suitable for colonizing these blacks. This committee recommended in its report that the blacks be colonized in Ohio, Indiana and Illinois.

The yearly meeting, therefore, ordered the removal of such Negroes as fast as they were willing or as might be consistent with the profession of their sect, and instructed the agents effecting the removal to draw on the treasury for any sum not exceeding two hundred dollars to defray expenses. An increasing number reached these States every year but, owing to the inducements offered by the American Colonization Society, some of them went to Liberia. When Liberia, however, developed into every thing but a haven of rest, the number sent to the settlements in the Northwest greatly increased.

The quarterly meeting succeeded in sending to the West 133 Negroes, including 23 free blacks and slaves given up because they were connected by marriage with those to be transplanted. The Negro colonists seemed to prefer Indiana. They went in three companies and with suitable young Friends to whom were executed powers of attorney to manumit, set free, settle and bind them out. Thirteen carts and wagons were bought for these three companies; $1,250 was furnished for their traveling expenses and clothing, the whole cost amounting to $2,490. It was planned to send forty or fifty to Long Island and twenty to the interior of Pennsylvania, but they failed to prosper and reports concerning them stamped them as destitute and deplorably ignorant. Those who went to Ohio and Indiana, however, did well.

Later we receive another interesting account of this exodus. David White led a company of fifty-three into the West, thirty-eight of whom belonged to Friends, five to a member who had ordered that they be taken West at his expense. Six of these slaves belonged to Samuel Lawrence, a Negro slaveholder, who had purchased himself and family. White pathetically reports the case of four of the women who had married slave husbands and had twenty children for the possession of whom the Friends had to stand a lawsuit in the courts. The women had decided to leave their husbands behind but the thought of separation so tormented them that they made an effort to secure their liberty. Upon appealing to their masters for terms the owners, somewhat moved by compassion, sold them for one half of their value. White then went West and left four in Chillicothe, twenty-three in

Leesburg and twenty-six in Wayne County, Indiana, without encountering any material difficulty.

Others had thought of this plan but the Quakers actually carried it out on a small scale. Here we see again not only their desire to have the Negroes emancipated but the vital interest of the Quakers in success of the blacks, for members of this sect not only liberated their slaves but sold out their own holdings in the South and moved with these freedmen into the North. Quakers who then lived in free States offered fugitives material assistance by open and clandestine methods. The most prominent leader developed by the movement was Levi Coffin, whose daring deeds in behalf of the fugitives made him the reputed President of the Underground Railroad. Most of the Quaker settlements of Negroes with which he was connected were made in what is now Hamilton, Howard, Wayne, Randolph, Vigo, Gibson, Grant, Rush, and Tipton Counties, Indiana, and Darke County, Ohio.

The promotion of this movement by the Quakers was well on its way by 1815 and was not materially checked until the fifties when the operations of the drastic fugitive slave law interfered, and even then the movement had gained such momentum and the execution of that mischievous measure had produced in the North so much reaction like that expressed in the personal liberty laws, that it could not be stopped. The Negroes found homes in Western New York, Western Pennsylvania and throughout the Northwest Territory. The Negro population of York, Harrisburg and Philadelphia rapidly increased. A settlement of Negroes developed at Sandy Lake in Northwestern Pennsylvania and there was another near Berlin Cross Roads in Ohio. A group of Negroes migrating to this same State found homes in the Van Buren Township of Shelby County. A more significant settlement in the State was made by Samuel Gist, an Englishman possessing extensive plantations in Hanover, Amherst, and Henrico Counties, Virginia. He provided in his will that his slaves should be freed and sent to the North. He further provided that the revenue from his plantation the last year of his life be applied in building schoolhouses and churches for their accommodation, and "that all money coming to him in Virginia be set aside for the employment of ministers and teachers to instruct them." In 1818, Wickham, the executor of his estate, purchased land and established these Negroes in what was called the Upper and Lower Camps of Brown County.

Augustus Wattles, a Quaker from Connecticut, made a settlement in Mercer County, Ohio, early in the nineteenth century. In the winter of 1833-4, he providentially became acquainted with the colored people of Cincinnati, finding there about "4,000 totally ignorant of every thing calculated to make good citizens." As most of them had been slaves, excluded from every avenue of moral and mental improvement, he established for them a school which he maintained for two years. He then proposed to these Negroes to go into the country and purchase land to remove them "from those contaminating influences which had so long crushed them in our cities and villages." They consented on the condition that he would accompany them and teach school. He travelled through Canada, Michigan and Indiana, looking for a suitable location, and finally selected for settlement a place in Mercer County, Ohio. In 1835, he made the first purchase of land there for this purpose and before 1838 Negroes had bought there about 30,000 acres, at the earnest appeal of this benefactor, who had travelled into almost every neighborhood of the blacks in the State, and laid before them the benefits of a permanent home for themselves and of education for their children.

This settlement was further increased in 1858 by the manumitted slaves of John Harper of North Carolina. John Randolph of Roanoke endeavored to establish his slaves as freemen in this county but the Germans who had settled in that community a little ahead of them started such a disturbance that Randolph's executor could not carry out his plan, although he had purchased a large tract of land there. It was necessary to send these freemen to Miami County. Theodoric H. Gregg of Dinwiddie County, Virginia, liberated his slaves in 1854 and sent them to Ohio. Nearer to the Civil War, when public opinion was proscribing the uplift of Negroes in Kentucky, Noah Spears secured near Xenia, Greene County, Ohio, a small parcel of land for sixteen of his former bondsmen in 1856. Other freedmen found their way to this community in later years and it became so prosperous that it was selected as the site of Wilberforce University.

This transplantation extended into Michigan. With the help of persons philanthropically inclined there sprang up a flourishing group of Negroes in Detroit. Early in the nineteenth century they began to acquire property and to provide for the education of their children. Their record was such as to merit the encomiums of their fellow white citizens. In later years this group in Detroit was increased by the operation of laws hostile to free Negroes in the South in that life for this class not only became intolerable but necessitated their expatriation. Because of the Virginia drastic laws and especially that of 1838 prohibiting the return to that State of such Negro students as had been accustomed to go North to attend school, after they were denied this privilege at home, the father of Richard DeBaptiste and Marie Louis More, the mother of Fannie M. Richards, led a colony of free Negroes from Fredericksburg to Detroit. And for about similar reasons the father of Robert A. Pelham conducted others from Petersburg, Virginia, in 1859. One Saunders, a planter of Cabell County, West Virginia, liberated his slaves some years later and furnished them homes among the Negroes settled in Cass County, Michigan, about ninety miles east of Chicago, and ninety-five miles west of Detroit.

This settlement had become attractive to fugitive slaves and freedmen because the Quakers settled there welcomed them on their way to freedom and in some cases encouraged them to remain among them. When the increase of fugitives was rendered impossible during the fifties when the Fugitive Slave Law was being enforced, there was still a steady growth due to the manumission of slaves by sympathetic and benevolent masters in the South. Most of these Negroes settled in Calvin Township, in that county, so that of the 1,376 residing there in 1860, 795 were established in this district, there being only 580 whites dispersed among them. The Negro settlers did not then obtain control of the government but they early purchased land to the extent of several thousand acres and developed into successful small farmers. Being a little more prosperous than the average Negro community in the North, the Cass County settlement not only attracted Negroes fleeing from hardships in the South but also those who had for some years unsuccessfully endeavored to establish themselves in other communities on free soil.

These settlements were duplicated a little farther west in Illinois. Edward Coles, a Virginian, who in 1818 emigrated to Illinois, of which he later served as Governor and as liberator from slavery, settled his slaves in that commonwealth. He brought them to Edwardsville, where they constituted a community known as "Coles' Negroes." There was another community of Negroes in Illinois in what is now called Brooklyn situated north of East St.

Louis. This town was a center of some consequence in the thirties. It became a station of the Underground Railroad on the route to Alton and to Canada. As all of the Negroes who emerged from the South did not go farther into the North, the black population of the town gradually grew despite the fact that slave hunters captured and reenslaved many of the Negroes who settled there.

These settlements together with favorable communities of sympathetic whites promoted the migration of the free Negroes and fugitives from the South by serving as centers offering assistance to those fleeing to the free States and to Canada. The fugitives usually found friends in Philadelphia, Columbia, Pittsburgh, Elmira, Rochester, Buffalo, Gallipolis, Portsmouth, Akron, Cincinnati, and Detroit. They passed on the way to freedom through Columbia, Philadelphia, Elizabethtown and by way of sea to New York and Boston, from which they proceeded to permanent settlements in the North.

In the West, the migration of the blacks was further facilitated by the peculiar geographic condition in that the

Appalachian highland, extending like a peninsula into the South, had a natural endowment which produced a class of white citizens hostile to the institution of slavery. These mountaineers coming later to the colonies had to go to the hills and mountains because the first comers from Europe had taken up the land near the sea. Being of the German and Scotch-Irish Presbyterian stock, they had ideals differing widely from those of the seaboard slaveholders. The mountaineers believed in "civil liberty in fee simple, and an open road to civil honors, secured to the poorest and feeblest members of society." The eastern element had for their ideal a government of interests for the people. They believed in liberty but that of kings, lords, and commons, not of all the people.

Settled along the Appalachian highland, these new stocks continued to differ from those dwelling near the sea, especially on the slavery question. The natural endowment of the mountainous section made slavery there unprofitable and the mountaineers bore it grievously that they were attached to commonwealths dominated by the radical pro-slavery element of the South, who sacrificed all other interests to safeguard those of the peculiar institution. There developed a number of clashes in all of the legislatures and constitutional conventions of the Southern States along the Atlantic, but in every case the defenders of the interests of slavery won.

When, therefore, slaves with the assistance of anti-slavery mountaineers began to escape to the free States, they had little difficulty in making their way through the Appalachian region, where the love of freedom had so set the people against slavery that although some of them yielded to the inevitable sin, they never made any systematic effort to protect it.

The development of the movement in these mountains was more than interesting. During the first quarter of the nineteenth century there were many ardent anti-slavery leaders in the mountains. These were not particularly interested in the Negro but were determined to keep that soil for freedom that the settlers might there realize the ideals for which they had left their homes in Europe. When the industrial revolution with the attendant rise of the plantation cotton culture made abolition in the South improbable, some of them became colonizationists, hoping to destroy the institution through deportation, which would remove the objection of certain masters who would free their slaves provided they were not left in the States to become a public charge. Some of this sentiment continued in the mountains even until the Civil War. The highlanders, therefore, found themselves involved in a continuous embroglio because they were not moved by reactionary influences which were unifying the South for its bold effort to make slavery a national institution. The other members of the mountaineer anti-slavery group became attached to the Underground Railroad system, endeavoring by secret methods to place on free soil a sufficiently large number of fugitives to show a decided diminution in the South. John Brown, who communicated with the South through these mountains, thought that his work would be a success, if he could change the situation in one county in each of these States.

The lines along which these Underground Railroad operators moved connected naturally with the Quaker settlements established in free States and the favorable sections in the Appalachian region. Many of these workers were Quakers who had already established settlements of slaves on estates which they had purchased in the Northwest Territory. Among these were John Rankin, James Gilliland, Jesse Lockehart, Robert Dobbins, Samuel Crothers, Hugh L. Fullerton, and William Dickey. Thus they connected the heart of the South with the avenues to freedom in the North. There were routes extending from this section into Ohio, Indiana, Illinois and Pennsylvania. Over the Ohio and Kentucky route culminating chiefly in Cleveland, Sandusky and Detroit, however, more fugitives made their way to freedom than through any other avenue, partly too because they found the limestone caves very helpful for hiding by day. These operations extended even through Tennessee into northern Georgia and Alabama. Dillingham, Josiah Henson and Harriet Tubman used these routes to deliver many a Negro from slavery.

The opportunity thus offered to help the oppressed brought forward a class of anti-slavery men, who went beyond the limit of merely expressing their horror of the evil. They believed that something should be done "to deliver the poor that cry and to direct the wanderer in the right way." Translating into action what had long been restricted to academic discussion, these philanthropic workers ushered in a new era in the uplift of the blacks, making abolition more of a reality. The abolition element of the North then could no longer be considered an insignificant minority advocating a hopeless cause but a factor in drawing from the South a part of its slave population and at the same time offering asylum to the free Negroes whom the southerners considered undesirable. Prominent among those who aided this migration in various ways were Benjamin Lundy of Tennessee and James G. Birney, a former slaveholder of Huntsville, Alabama, who manumitted his slaves and apprenticed and educated some of them in Ohio.

This exodus of the Negroes to the free States promoted the migration of others of their race to Canada, a more congenial part beyond the borders of the United States. The movement from the free States into Canada, moreover, was contemporary with that from the South to the free States as will be evidenced by the fact that 15,000 of the 60,000 Negroes in Canada in 1860 were free born. As Detroit was the chief gateway for them to Canada, most of these refugees settled in towns of Southern Ontario not far from that city. These were Dawn, Colchester, Elgin, Dresden, Windsor, Sandwich,

Bush, Wilberforce, Hamilton, St. Catherines, Chatham, Riley, Anderton, London, Malden and Gonfield. And their coming to Canada was not checked even by request from their enemies that they be turned away from that country as undesirables, for some of the white people there welcomed and assisted them. Canadians later experienced a change in their attitude toward these refugees but these British Americans never made the life of the Negro there so intolerable as was the case in some of the free States.

It should be observed here that this movement, unlike the exodus of the Negroes of today, affected an unequal distribution of the enlightened Negroes. Those who are fleeing from the South today are largely laborers seeking economic opportunities. The motive at work in the mind of the antebellum refugee was higher. In 1840 there were more intelligent blacks in the South than in the North but not so after 1850, despite the vigorous execution of the Fugitive Slave Law in some parts of the North. While the free Negro population of the slave States increased only 23,736 from 1850 to 1860, that of the free States increased 29,839. In the South, only Delaware, Maryland and North Carolina showed a noticeable increase in the number of free persons of color during the decade immediately preceding the Civil War. This element of the population had only slightly increased in Alabama, Kentucky, Missouri, Tennessee, Virginia, Louisiana, South Carolina and the District of Columbia. The number of free Negroes of Florida remained constant. Those of Arkansas, Mississippi and Texas diminished. In the North, of course, the migration had caused the tendency to be in the other direction. With the exception of Maine, New Hampshire, Vermont and New York which had about the same free colored population in 1860 as they had in 1850 there was a general increase in the number of Negroes in the free States. Ohio led in this respect, having had during this period an increase of 11,394. A glance at the table on the accompanying page will show in detail the results of this migration.

STATISTICS OF THE FREE COLORED POPULATION OF THE UNITED STATES

State Population	
1850 1860	
Alabama	2,265 2,690
Arkansas…	608 144
California…	962 4,086
Connecticut…	7,693 8,627
Delaware…	18,073 19,829
Florida	932 932
Georgia	2,931 3,500
Illinois…	5,436 7,628
Indiana	11,262 11,428
Iowa	333 1,069
Kentucky	10,011 10,684
Louisiana	17,462 18,647
Maine…	1,356 1,327
Kansas…	625
Maryland…	74,723 83,942
Massachusetts	9,064 9,602
Michigan	2,583 6,797
Minnesota	259
Mississippi	930 773
Missouri	2,618 3,572

New Hampshire… 520 494

New Jersey	23,810 25,318
New York	49,069 49,005
North Carolina	27,463 30,463
Ohio	25,279 36,673
Oregon	128
Pennsylvania	53,626 56,949
Rhode Island...	3,670 3,952
South Carolina	8,960 9,914
Tennessee...	6,422 7,300
Texas...	397 355
Vermont...	718 709
Virginia...	54,333 58,042
Wisconsin	635 1,171
Territories: Colorado...	46
Dakota	0
District of Columbia...	10,059 11,131
Minnesota	39
Nebraska	67
Nevada	45
New Mexico	207 85
Oregon	24
Utah	22 30
Washington	30
Total	434,495 488,070

CHAPTER 3. FIGHTING IT OUT ON FREE SOIL

How, then, was this increasing influx of refugees from the South to be received in the free States? In the older Northern States where there could be no danger of an Africanization of a large district, the coming of the Negroes did not cause general excitement, though at times the feeling in certain localities was sufficient to make one think so. Fearing that the immigration of the Negroes into the North might so increase their numbers as to make them constitute a rather important part in the community, however, some free States enacted laws to restrict the privileges of the blacks.

Free Negroes had voted in all the colonies except Georgia and South Carolina, if they had the property qualification; but after the sentiment attendant upon the struggle for the rights of man had passed away there set in a reaction. Delaware, Maryland, Virginia and Kentucky disfranchised all Negroes not long after the Revolution. They voted in North Carolina until 1835, when the State, feeling that this privilege of one class of Negroes might affect the enslavement of the other, prohibited it. The Northern States, following in their wake, set up the same barriers against the blacks.

They were disfranchised in New Jersey in 1807, in Connecticut in 1814, and in Pennsylvania in 1838. In 1811 New York passed an act requiring the production of certificates of freedom from blacks or mulattoes offering to vote. The second constitution, adopted in 1823, provided that no man of color, unless he had been for three years a citizen of that State and for one year next preceding any election, should be seized and possessed of a freehold estate, should be allowed to vote, although this qualification was not required of the whites. An act of 1824 relating to the government of the Stockbridge Indians provided that no Negro or mulatto should vote in their councils.

That increasing prejudice was to a great extent the result of the immigration into the North of Negroes in the rough, was nowhere better illustrated than in Pennsylvania. Prior to 1800, and especially after 1780, when the State provided for gradual emancipation, there was little race prejudice in Pennsylvania. When the reactionary legislation of the South made life intolerable for the Negroes, debasing them to the plane of beasts, many of the free people of color from Virginia, Maryland and Delaware moved or escaped into Pennsylvania like a steady stream during the next sixty years. As these Negroes tended to concentrate in towns and cities, they caused the supply of labor to exceed the demand, lowering the wages of some and driving out of employment a number of others who became paupers and consequently criminals. There set in too an intense struggle between the black and white laborers, immensely accelerating the growth of race prejudice, especially when the abolitionists and Quakers were giving Negroes industrial training.

The first exhibition of this prejudice was seen among the lower classes of white people, largely Irish and Germans, who, devoted to menial labor, competed directly with the Negroes. It did not require a long time, however, for this feeling to react on the higher classes of whites where Negroes settled in large groups. A strong protest arose from the menace of Negro paupers. An attempt was made in 1804 to compel free Negroes to maintain those that might become a public charge. In 1813 the mayor, aldermen and citizens of Philadelphia asked that free Negroes be taxed to support their poor. Two Philadelphia representatives in the Pennsylvania Legislature had a committee appointed in 1815 to consider the advisability of preventing the immigration of Negroes. One of the causes then at work there was that the black population had recently increased to four thousand in Philadelphia and more than four thousand others had come into the city since the previous registration.

They were arriving much faster than they could be assimilated. The State of Pennsylvania had about exterminated slavery by 1840, having only 40 slaves that year and only a few hundred at any time after 1810. Many of these, of course, had not had time to make their way in life as freedmen. To show how much the rapid migration to that city aggravated the situation under these circumstances one needs but note the statistics of the increase of the free people of color in that State. There were only 22,492 such persons in Pennsylvania in 1810, but in 1820 there were 30,202, and in 1830 as many as 37,930. This number increased to 47,854 by 1840, to 53,626 by 1850, and to 56,949 by 1860. The undesirable aspect of the situation was that most of the migrating blacks came in crude form. "On arriving," therefore, says a contemporary, "they abandoned themselves to all manner of debauchery and dissipation to the great annoyance of many citizens."

Thereafter followed a number of clashes developing finally into a series of riots of a grave nature. Innocent Negroes, attacked at first for purposes of sport and later for sinister designs, were often badly beaten in the streets or even cut with knives. The offenders were not punished and if the Negroes defended themselves they were usually severely penalized. In 1819 three white women stoned a woman of color to death. A few youths entered a Negro church in Philadelphia in 1825 and by throwing pepper to give rise to suffocating fumes caused a panic which resulted in the death of several Negroes. When the citizens of New Haven, Connecticut, arrayed themselves in 1831 against the plan to establish in that city a Negro manual labor college, there was held in Philadelphia a meeting which passed resolutions enthusiastically endorsing this effort to rid the community of the evil of the immigration of free Negroes. There arose also the custom of driving Negroes away from Independence Square on the Fourth of July because they were neither considered nor desired as a part of the body politic.

It was thought that in the state of feeling of the thirties that the Negro would be annihilated. De Tocqueville also observed that the Negroes were more detested in the free States than in those where they were held as slaves. There had been such a reaction since 1800 that no positions of consequence were open to Negroes, however well educated they might be, and the education of the blacks which was once vigorously prosecuted there became unpopular. This was especially true of Harrisburg and Philadelphia but by no means confined to large cities. The Philadelphia press said nothing in behalf of the race. It was generally thought that freedom had not been an advantage to the Negro and that instead of making progress they had filled jails and almshouses and multiplied pest holes to afflict the cities with disease and crime.

The Negroes of York carefully worked out in 1803 a plan to burn the city. Incendiaries set on fire a number of houses, eleven of which were destroyed, whereas there were other attempts at a general destruction of the city. The authorities arrested a number of Negroes but ran the risk of having the jail broken open by their sympathizing fellowmen. After a reign of terror for half a week, order was restored and twenty of the accused were convicted of arson.

In 1820 there occurred so many conflagrations that a vigilance committee was organized. Whether or not the Negroes were guilty of the crime is not known but numbers of them left either on account of the fear of punishment or because of the indignities to which they were subjected.

Numerous petitions, therefore, came before the legislature to stop the immigration of Negroes. It was proposed in 1840 to tax all free Negroes to assist them in getting out of the State for colonization. The citizens of Lehigh County asked the authorities in 1830 to expel all Negroes and persons of color found in the State. Another petition prayed that they be deprived of the freedom of movement. Bills embodying these ideas were frequently considered but they were never passed.

Stronger opposition than this, however, was manifested in the form of actual outbreaks on a large scale in Philadelphia. The immediate cause of this first real clash was the abolition agitation in the city in 1834 following the exciting news of other such disturbances a few months prior to this date in several northern cities. A group of boys started the riot by destroying a Negro resort. A mob then proceeded to the Negro district, where white and colored men engaged in a fight with clubs and stones.

The next day the mob ruined the African Presbyterian Church and attacked some Negroes, destroying their property and beating them mercilessly. This riot continued for three days. A committee appointed to inquire into the causes of the riot reported that the aim of the rioters had been to make the Negroes go away because it was believed that their labor was depriving them of work and because the blacks had shielded criminals and had made such noise and disorder in their churches as to make them a nuisance. It seemed that the most intelligent and well-to-do people of Philadelphia keenly felt it that the city had thus been disgraced, but the mob spirit continued.

The very next year was marked by the same sort of disorder. Because a half- witted Negro attempted to murder a white man, a large mob stirred up the city again. There was a repetition of the beating of Negroes and of the destruction of property while the police, as the year before, were so inactive as to give rise to the charge that they were accessories to the riot. In 1838 there occurred another outbreak which developed into an anti-abolition riot, as the public mind had been much exercised by the discussions of abolitionists and by their close social contact with the Negroes. The clash came on the seventeenth of May when Pennsylvania Hall, the center of abolition agitation, was burned. Fighting between the blacks and whites ensued the following night when the Colored Orphan Asylum was attacked and a Negro church burned. Order was finally restored for the good of all concerned, but that a majority of the people sympathized with the rioters was evidenced by the fact that the committee charged with investigating the disturbance reported that the mob was composed of strangers who could not be recognized. It is well to note here that this riot occurred the year the Negroes in Pennsylvania were disfranchised.

Following the example of Philadelphia, Pittsburgh had a riot in 1839 resulting in the maltreatment of a number of Negroes and the demolishing of some of their houses. When the Negroes of Philadelphia paraded the city in 1842, celebrating the abolition of slavery in the West Indies, there ensued a battle led by the whites who undertook to break up the procession. Along with the beating and killing of the usual number went also the destruction of the New African Hall and the Negro Presbyterian church. The grand jury charged with the inquiry into the causes reported that the procession was to be blamed. For several years thereafter the city remained quiet until 1849 when there occurred a raid on the blacks by the Killers of Moyamensing, using firearms with which many were wounded. This disturbance was finally quelled by aid of the militia.

These clashes sometimes reached farther north than the free States bordering on the slave commonwealths. Mobs broke up abolition meetings in the city of New York in 1834 when there were sent to Congress numerous petitions for the abolition of slavery. This mob even assailed such eminent citizens as Arthur and Lewis Tappan, mainly on account of their friendly attitude toward the Negroes. On October 21, 1834, the same feeling developed in Utica, where was to be held an anti-slavery meeting according to previous notice. The six hundred delegates who assembled there were warned to disband. A mob then organized itself and drove the delegates from the town. That same month the people of Palmyra, New York, held a meeting at which they adopted resolutions to the effect that owners of houses or tenements in that town occupied by blacks of the character complained of be requested to use all their rightful means to clear their premises of such occupants at the earliest possible period; and that it be recommended that such proprietors refuse to rent the same thereafter to any person of color whatever. In New York Negroes were excluded from places of amusement and public conveyances and segregated in places of worship. In the draft riots which occurred there in 1863, one of the aims of the mobs was to assassinate Negroes and to destroy their property. They burned the Colored Orphan Asylum of that city and hanged Negroes to lamp-posts.

The situation in parts of New England was not much better. For fear of the evils of an increasing population of free persons of color the people of Canaan, New Hampshire, broke up the Noyes Academy because it decided to admit Negro students, thinking that many of the race might thereby be encouraged to come to that State. When Prudence Crandall established in Canterbury, Connecticut, an academy to which she decided to admit Negroes, the mayor, selectmen and citizens of the city protested, and when their protests failed to deter this heroine, they induced the legislature to enact a special law covering the case and invoked the measure to have Prudence Crandall imprisoned because she would not desist. This very law and the arguments upholding it justified the drastic measure on the ground that an increase in the colored population would be an injury to the people of that State.

In the new commonwealths formed out of western territory, there was the same fear as to Negro domination and consequently there followed the wave of legislation intended in some cases not only to withhold from the Negro settlers the exercise of the rights of citizenship but to discourage and even to prevent them from coming into their territory. The question as to what should be done with the Negro was early an issue in Ohio. It came up in the constitutional convention of 1803, and provoked some discussion, but that body considered it sufficient to settle the matter for the time being by merely leaving the Negroes, Indians and foreigners out of the pale of the newly organized body politic by conveniently incorporating the word white throughout the constitution. It was soon evident, however, that the matter had not been settled, and the legislature of 1804 had to give serious consideration to the immigration of Negroes into that State. It was, therefore, enacted that no Negro or mulatto should remain there permanently, unless he could furnish a certificate of freedom issued by some court, that all Negroes in that commonwealth should be registered before the following June, and that no man should employ a Negro who failed to comply with these conditions. Should one be detected in hiring, harboring or hindering the capture of a fugitive black, he was liable to a fine of $50 and his master could recover pay for the service of his slave to the amount of fifty cents a day.

As this legislature did not meet the demands of those who desired further to discourage Negro immigration, the Legislature of 1807 was induced to enact a law to the effect that no Negro should be permitted to settle in Ohio, unless he could within 20 days give a bond to the amount of $500 for his good behavior and assurance that he would not become a public charge. This measure provided also for raising the fine for concealing a fugitive from $50 to $100, one half of which should go to the person upon the testimony of whom the conviction should be secured. Negro evidence in a case to which a white was a party was declared illegal. In 1830 Negroes were excluded from service in the State militia, in 1831 they were deprived of the privilege of serving on juries, and in 1838 they were denied the right of having their children educated at the expense of the State.

In Indiana the situation was worse than in Ohio. We have already noted above how the settlers in the southern part endeavored to make that a slave State. When that had, after all but being successful, seemed impossible the State enacted laws to prevent or discourage the influx of free Negroes and to restrict the privileges of those already there. In 1824 a stringent law for the return of fugitives was passed. The expulsion of free

Negroes was a matter of concern and in 1831 it was provided that unless they could give bond for their behavior and support they could be removed. Otherwise the county overseers could hire out such Negroes to the highest bidder. Negroes were not allowed to attend schools maintained at the public expense, might not give evidence against a white man and could not intermarry with white persons. They might, however, serve as witnesses against Negroes.

In the same way the free Negroes met discouragement in Illinois. They suffered from all the disabilities imposed on their class in Ohio and Indiana and were denied the right to sue for their liberty in the courts. When there arose many abolitionists who encouraged the coming of the fugitives from labor in the South, one element of the citizens of Illinois unwilling to accept this unusual influx of members of another race passed the drastic law of 1853 prohibiting the immigration. It provided for the prosecution of any person bringing a Negro into the State and also for arresting and fining any Negro $50, should he appear there and remain longer than ten days. If he proved to be unable to pay the fine, he could be sold to any person who could pay the cost of the trial.

In Michigan the situation was a little better but, with the waves of hostile legislation then sweeping over the new commonwealths, Michigan was not allowed to constitute altogether an exception. Some of this intense feeling found expression in the form of a law hostile to the Negro, this being the act of 1827, which provided for the registration of all free persons of color and for the exclusion from the territory of all blacks who could not produce a certificate to the effect that they were free. Free persons of color were also required to file bonds with one or more freehold sureties in the penal sum of $500 for their good behavior, and the bondsmen were expected to provide for their maintenance, if they failed to support themselves. Failure to comply with this law meant expulsion from the territory.

The opposition to the Negroes immigrating into the new West was not restricted to the enactment of laws which in some cases were never enforced. Several communities took the law into their own hands. During these years when the Negroes were seeking freedom in the Northwest Territory and when free blacks were being established there by philanthropists, it seemed to the southern uplanders fleeing from slavery in the border States and foreigners seeking fortunes in the new world that they might possibly be crowded out of this new territory by the Negroes.

Frequent clashes, therefore, followed after they had passed through a period of toleration and dependence on the execution of the hostile laws. The clashes of the greatest consequences occurred in the Northwest Territory where a larger number of uplanders from the South had gone, some to escape the ill effects of slavery, and others to hold slaves if possible, and when that seemed impossible, to exclude the blacks altogether. This persecution of the Negroes received also the hearty cooperation of the foreign element, who, being an undeveloped class, had to do menial labor in competition with the blacks. The feeling of the foreigners was especially mischievous for the reasons that they were, like the Negroes, at first settled in large numbers in urban communities.

Generally speaking, the feeling was like that exhibited by the Germans in Mercer County, Ohio. The citizens of this frontier community, in registering their protest against the settling of Negroes there, adopted the following resolutions:

Resolved, That we will not live among Negroes, as we have settled here first, we have fully determined that we will resist the settlement of blacks and mulattoes in this county to the full extent of our means, the bayonet not excepted.

Resolved, That the blacks of this county be, and they are hereby respectfully requested to leave the county on or before the first day of March, 1847; and in the case of their neglect or refusal to comply with this request, we pledge ourselves to remove them, peacefully if we can, forcibly if we must.

Resolved, That we who are here assembled, pledge ourselves not to employ or trade with any black or mulatto person, in any manner whatever, or permit them to have any grinding done at our mills, after the first day of January next.

In 1827 there arose a storm of protest on the occasion of the settling of seventy freedmen in Lawrence County, Ohio, by a philanthropic master of Pittsylvania County, Virginia. On Black Friday, January 1, 1830, eighty Negroes were driven out of Portsmouth, Ohio, at the request of one or two hundred white citizens set forth in an urgent memorial. So many Negroes during these years concentrated at Cincinnati that the laboring element forced the execution of the almost dead law requiring free Negroes to produce certificates and give bonds for their behavior and support. A mob attacked the homes of the blacks, killed a number of them, and forced twelve hundred others to leave for Canada West, where they established the settlement known as Wilberforce.

In 1836 another mob attacked and destroyed there the press of James G. Birney, the editor of the Philanthropist, because of the encouragement his abolitionist organ gave to the immigrating Negroes. But in 1841 came a decidedly systematic effort on the part of foreigners and proslavery sympathizers to kill off and drive out the Negroes who were becoming too well established in that city and who were giving offense to white men who desired to deal with them as Negroes were treated in the South. The city continued in this excited state for about a week. There were brought into play in the upheaval the police of the city and the State militia before the shooting of the Negroes and burning of their homes could be checked. So far as is known, no white men were punished, although a few of them were arrested. Some Negroes were committed to prison during the fray. They were thereafter either discharged upon producing certificates of nativity or giving bond or were indefinitely held.

In southern Indiana and Illinois the same condition obtained. Observing the situation in Indiana, a contributor of Niles Register remarked, in 1818, upon the arrival there of sixty or seventy liberated Negroes sent by the society of Friends of North Carolina, that they were a species of population that was not acceptable to the people of that State, "nor indeed to any other, whether free or slaveholding, for they cannot rise and become like other men, unless in countries where their own color predominates, but must always remain a degraded and inferior class of persons without the hope of much bettering their condition."

The Indiana Farmer, voicing the sentiment of that same community, regretted the increase of this population that seemed to be enlarging the number sent to that territory. The editor insisted that the community which enjoys the benefits of the blacks' labor should also suffer all the consequences. Since the people of Indiana derived no advantage from slavery, he begged that they be excused from its inconveniences. Most of the blacks that migrated there, moreover, possessed, thought he, "feelings quite unprepared to make good citizens. A sense of inferiority early impressed on their minds, destitute of every thing but bodily power and having no character to lose, and no prospect of acquiring one, even did they know its value, they are prepared for the commission of any act, when the prospect of evading punishment is favorable."

With the exception of such centers as Eden, Upper Alton, Bellville and Chicago, this antagonistic attitude was general also in the State of Illinois. The Negroes were despised, abused and maltreated as persons who had no rights that the white man should respect. Even in Detroit, Michigan, in 1833 a fracas was started by an attack on Negroes. Because a courageous group of them had effected the rescue and escape of one Thornton Blackburn and his wife who had been arrested by the sheriff as alleged fugitives from Kentucky, the citizens invoked the law of 1827, to require free Negroes to produce a certificate and furnish bonds for their behavior and support. The anti-slavery sentiment there, however, was so strong that the law was not long rigidly enforced. And so it was in several other parts of the West which, however, were exceptional.

CHAPTER 4. COLONIZATION AS A REMEDY FOR MIGRATION

Because of these untoward circumstances consequent to the immigration of free Negroes and fugitives into the North, their enemies, and in some cases their well-intentioned friends, advocated the diversion of these elements to foreign soil. Benezet and Brannagan had the idea of settling the Negroes on the public lands in the West largely to relieve the situation in the North. Certain anti-slavery men of Kentucky, as we have observed, recommended the same. But this was hardly advocated at all by the farseeing white men after the close of the first quarter of the nineteenth century. It was by that time very clear that white men would want to occupy all lands within the present limits of the United States. Few statesmen dared to encourage migration to Canada because the large number of fugitives who had already escaped there had attached to that region the stigma of being an asylum for fugitives from the slave States.

The most influential people who gave thought to this question finally decided that the colonization of the Negro in Africa was the only solution of the problem. The plan of African colonization appealed more generally to the people of both North and South than the other efforts, which, at best, could do no more than to offer local or temporary relief. The African colonizationists proceeded on the basis that the Negroes had no chance for racial development in this country. They could secure no kind of honorable employment, could not associate with congenial white friends whose minds and pursuits might operate as a stimulus upon their industry and could not rise to the level of the successful professional or business men found around them. In short, they must ever be hewers of wood and drawers of water.

To emphasize further the necessity of emigration to Africa the advocates of deportation to foreign soil generally referred to the condition of the migrating Negroes as a case in evidence. "So long," said one, "as you must sit, stand, walk, ride, dwell, eat and sleep here and the Negro there, he cannot be free in any part of the country." This idea working through the minds of northern men, who had for years thought merely of the injustice of slavery, began to change their attitude toward the abolitionists who had never undertaken to solve the problem of the blacks who were seeking refuge in the North. Many thinkers controlling public opinion then gave audience to the colonizationists and circles once closed to them were thereafter opened.

There was, therefore, a tendency toward a more systematic effort than had hitherto characterized the endeavors of the colonizationists. The objects of their philanthropy were not to be stolen away and hurried off to an uncongenial land for the oppressed. They were in accordance with the exigencies of their new situation to be prepared by instruction in mechanic arts, agriculture, science and Biblical literature that some might lead in the higher pursuits and others might skilfully serve their fellows. Private enterprise was at first depended on to carry out the schemes but it soon became evident that a better method was necessary. Finally out of the proposals of various thinkers and out of the actual colonization feats of Paul Cuffé, a Negro, came a national meeting for this purpose, held in Washington, December, 1816, and the organization of the American Colonization Society. This meeting was attended by some of the most prominent men in the United States, among whom were Henry Clay, Francis

S. Key, Bishop William Meade, John Randolph and Judge

Bushrod Washington.

The American Colonization Society, however, failed to facilitate the movement of the free Negro from the South and did not promote the general welfare of the race. The reasons for these failures are many. In the first place, the society was all things to all men. To the anti-slavery man whose ardor had been dampened by the meagre results obtained by his agitation, the scheme was the next best thing to remove the objections of slaveholders who had said they would emancipate their bondsmen, if they could be assured of their being deported to foreign soil. To the radical proslavery man and to the northerner hating the Negro it was well adapted to rid the country of the free persons of color whom they regarded as the pariahs of society. Furthermore, although the Colonization Society became seemingly popular and the various States organized branches of it and raised money to promote the movement, the slaveholders as a majority never reached the position of parting with their slaves and the country would not take such radical action as to compel free Negroes to undergo expatriation when militant abolitionists were fearlessly denouncing the scheme.

The free people of color themselves were not only not anxious to go but bore it grievously that any one should even suggest that they should be driven from the country in which they were born and for the independence of which their fathers had died. They held indignation meetings throughout the North to denounce the scheme as a selfish policy inimical to the interests of the people of color. Branded thus as the inveterate foe of the blacks both slave and free, the American Colonization Society effected the deportation of only such Negroes as southern masters felt disposed to emancipate from time to time and a few others induced to go. As the industrial revolution early changed the aspect of the economic situation in the South so as to make slavery seemingly profitable, few masters ever thought of liberating their slaves.

Scarcely any intelligent Negroes except those who, for economic or religious reasons were interested, availed themselves of this opportunity to go to the land of their ancestors. From the reports of the Colonization Society we learn that from 1820 to 1833 only 2,885 Negroes were sent to Africa by the Society. Furthermore, more than 2,700 of this number were taken from the slave States, and about two thirds of these were slaves manumitted on the condition that they would emigrate. Later statistics show the same tendency. By 1852, 7,836 had been deported from the United States to Liberia. 2,720 of these were born free, 204 purchased their freedom, 3,868 were emancipated in view of their going to Liberia and 1,044 were liberated Africans returned by the United States Government. Considering the fact that there were 434,495 free persons of color in this country in 1850 and 488,070 in 1860, the colonizationists saw that the very element of the population which the movement was intended to send out of the country had increased rather than decreased. It is clear, then, that the American Colonization Society, though regarded as a factor to play an important part in promoting the exodus of the free Negroes to foreign soil, was an inglorious failure.

Colonization in other quarters, however, was not abandoned. A colony of Negroes in Texas was contemplated in 1833 prior to the time when the republic became independent of Mexico, as slavery was not at first assured in that State. The New York Commercial Advertiser had no objection to the enterprise but felt that there were natural obstacles such as a more expensive conveyance than that to Monrovia, the high price of land in that country, the Catholic religion to which Negroes were not accustomed to conform, and their lack of knowledge of the Spanish language. The editor observed that some who had emigrated to Hayti a few years before became discontented because they did not know the language. Louisiana, a slave

State, moreover, would not suffer near its borders a free Negro republic to serve as an asylum for refugees. The Richmond Whig saw the actual situation in dubbing the scheme as chimerical for the reason that a more unsuitable country for the blacks did not exist. Socially and politically it would never suit the Negroes. Already a great number of adventurers from the United States had gone to Texas and fugitives from justice from Mexico, a fierce, lawless and turbulent class, would give the Negroes little chance there, as the Negroes could not contend with the Spaniard and the Creole.

The editor believed that an inferior race could never exist in safety surrounded by a superior one despising them. Colonization in Africa was then urged and the efforts of the blacks to go elsewhere were characterized as doing mischief at every turn to defeat the "enlightened plan" for the amelioration of the Negroes.

It was still thought possible to induce the Negroes to go to some congenial foreign land, although few of them would agree to emigrate to Africa. Not a few Negroes began during the two decades immediately preceding the Civil War to think more favorably of African colonization and a still larger number, in view of the increasing disabilities fixed upon their class, thought of migrating to some country nearer to the United States. Much was said about Central America, but British Guiana and the West Indies proved to be the most inviting fields to the latter-day Negro colonizationists. This idea was by no means new, for Jefferson in his foresight had, in a letter to Governor Edward Coles, of Illinois, in 1814, shown the possibilities of colonization in the West Indies. He felt that because Santo Domingo had become an independent Negro republic it would offer a solution of the problem as to where the Negroes should be colonized. In this way these islands would become a sort of safety valve for the United States. He became more and more convinced that all the West Indies would remain in the hands of the people of color, and a total expulsion of the whites sooner or later would take place. It was high time, he thought, that Americans should foresee the bloody scenes which their children certainly, and possibly they themselves, would have to wade through.

The movement to the West Indies was accelerated by other factors. After the emancipation in those islands in the thirties, there had for some years been a dearth of labor. Desiring to enjoy their freedom and living in a climate where there was not much struggle for life, the freedmen either refused to work regularly or wandered about purposely from year to year. The islands in which sugar had once played a conspicuous part as the foundation of their industry declined and something had to be done to meet this exigency. In the forties and fifties, therefore, there came to the United States a number of labor agents whose aim was to set forth the inviting aspect of the situation in the West Indies so as to induce free Negroes to try their fortunes there. To this end meetings were held in Baltimore, Philadelphia, New York and Boston and even in some of the cities of the South, where these agents appealed to the free Negroes to emigrate.

Thus before the American Colonization Society had got well on its way toward accomplishing its purpose of deporting the Negroes to Africa the West Indies and British Guiana claimed the attention of free people of color in offering there unusual opportunities. After the consummation of British emancipation in those islands in 1838, the English nation came to he regarded by the Negroes of the United States as the exclusive friend of the race. The Negro press and church vied with each other in praising British emancipation as an act of philanthropy and pointed to the English dominions as an asylum for the oppressed. So disturbed were the whites by this growing feeling that riots broke out in northern cities on occasions of Negro celebrations of the anniversary of emancipation in the West Indies.

In view of these facts, the colonizationists had to redouble their efforts to defend their cause. They found it a little difficult to make a good case for Liberia, a land far away in an unhealthy climate so much unlike that of the West Indies and British Guiana, where Negroes had been declared citizens entitled to all privileges afforded by the government. The colonizationists could do no more than to express doubt that the Negroes would have there the opportunities for mental, moral and social betterment which were offered in Liberia. The promoters of the enterprise in Africa did not believe that the West Indian planters who had had emancipation forced upon them would accept blacks from the United States as their equals, nor that they, far from receiving the consideration of freedmen, would be there any more than menials. When told of the establishment of schools and churches for the improvement of the freedmen, the colonizationists replied that schools might be provided, but the planters could have no interest in encouraging education as they did not want an elevated class of people but bone and muscle. As an evidence of the truth of this statement it was asserted that newspapers of the country were filled with disastrous accounts of the falling off of crops and the scarcity of labor but had little to say about those forces instrumental in the uplift of the people.

An effort was made also to show that there would be no economic advantage in going to the British dominions. It was thought that as soon as the first demand for labor was supplied wages would be reduced, for no new plantations could be opened there as in a growing country like Liberia. It would be impossible, therefore, for the Negroes immigrating there to take up land and develop a class of small farmers as they were doing in Africa.

Under such circumstances, they contended, the Negroes in the West Indies could not feel any of the "elevating influences of nationality of character," as the white men would limit the influence of the Negroes by retaining practically all of the wealth of the islands. The inducements, therefore, offered the free Negroes in the United States were merely intended to use them in supplying in the British dominions the need of men to do drudgery scarcely more elevating than the toil of slaves.

Determined to interest a larger number of persons in diverting the attention of the free Negroes from the West Indies, the colonizationists took higher ground. They asserted that the interests of the millions of white men in this country were then at stake, and even if it would be better for the three million Negroes of the country gradually to emigrate to the British dominions, it would eventually prove prejudicial to the interests of the United States. They showed how the Negroes immigrating into the West Indies would be made to believe that the refusal to extend to them here social and political equality was cruel oppression and the immigrants, therefore, would carry with them no good will to this country. When they arrived in the West Indies their circumstances would increase this hostility, alienate their affections and estrange them wholly from the United States. Taught to regard the British as the exclusive friends of their race, devoted to its elevation, they would become British in spirit. As such, these Negroes would be controlled by British influence and would increase the wealth and commerce of the British and as soldiers would greatly strengthen British power.

It was better, therefore, they argued, to direct the Negroes to Liberia, for those who went there with a feeling of hostility against the white people were placed in circumstances operating to remove that feeling, in that the kind solicitude for their welfare would be extended them in their new home so as to overcome their prejudices, win their confidence, and secure their attachment. Looking to this country as their fatherland and the home of their benefactors, the Liberians would develop a nation, taking the religion, customs and laws of this country as their models, marketing their produce in this country and purchasing our manufactures. In spite of its independence, therefore, Liberia would be American in feeling, language and interests, affording a means to get rid of a class undesirable here but desirable to us there in their power to extend American influence, trade and commerce.

Negroes migrated to the West Indies in spite of this warning and protest. Hayti, at first looked upon with fear of having a free Negro government near slaveholding States, became fixed in the minds of some as a desirable place for the colonization of free persons of color. This was due to the apparent natural advantages in soil, climate and the situation of the country over other places in consideration. It was thought that the island would support fourteen millions of people and that, once opened to immigration from the United States, it would in a few years fill up by natural increase. It was remembered that it was formerly the emporium of the Western World and that it supplied both hemispheres with sugar and coffee. It had rapidly recovered from the disaster of the French Revolution and lacked only capital and education which the United States under these circumstances could furnish. Furthermore, it was argued that something in this direction should be immediately done, as European nations then seeking to establish friendly relations with the islands, would secure there commercial advantages which the United States should have and could establish by sending to that island free Negroes especially devoted to agriculture.

In 1836, Z. Kingsley, a Florida planter, actually undertook to carry out such a plan on a small scale. He established on the northeast side of Hayti, near Port Plate, his son, George Kingsley, a well-educated colored man of industrious habits and uncorrupted morals, together with six "prime African men," slaves liberated for that express purpose. There he purchased for them 35,000 acres of land upon which they engaged in the production of crops indigenous to that soil.

Hayti, however, was not to be the only island to get consideration. In 1834 two hundred colored emigrants went from New York alone to Trinidad, under the superintendence and at the expense of planters of that island. It was later reported that every one of them found employment on the day of arrival and in one or two instances the most intelligent were placed as overseers at the salary of $500 per annum. No one received less than $1.00 a day and most of them earned $1.50. The Trinidad press welcomed these immigrants and spoke in the highest terms of the valuable services they rendered the country. Others followed from year to year. One of these Negroes appreciated so much this new field of opportunity that he returned and induced twenty intelligent free persons of color living in Annapolis, Maryland, also to emigrate to Trinidad.

The New York Sun reported in 1840 that 160 colored persons left Philadelphia for Trinidad. They had been hired by an eminent planter to labor on that island and they were encouraged to expect that they should have privileges which would make their residence desirable. The editor wished a few dozen Trinidad planters would come to that city on the same business and on a much larger scale. N.W. Pollard, agent of the Government of Trinidad, came to Baltimore in 1851 to make his appeal for emigrants, offering to pay all expenses. At a meeting held in Baltimore, in 1852, the parents of Mr.

Stanbury Boyce, now a retired merchant in Washington, District of Columbia, were also induced to go. They found there opportunities which they had never had before and well established themselves in their new home. The account which Mr. Boyce gives in a letter to the writer corroborates the newspaper reports as to the success of the enterprise.

The New York Journal of Commerce reported in 1841 that, according to advices received at New Orleans from Jamaica, there had arrived in that island fourteen Negro emigrants from the United States, being the first fruits of Mr. Barclay's mission to this country. A much larger number of Negroes were expected and various applications for their services had been received from respectable parties. The products of soil were reported as much reduced from former years and to meet its demand for labor some freedmen from Sierra Leone were induced to emigrate to that island in 1842. One Mr. Anderson, an agent of the government of Jamaica, contemplated visiting New York in 1851 to secure a number of laborers, tradesmen and agricultural settlers.

In the course of time, emigration to foreign lands interested a larger number of representative Negroes. At a national council called in 1853 to promote more effectively the amelioration of the colored people, the question of emigration and that only was taken up for serious consideration. But those who desired to introduce the question of Liberian colonization or who were especially interested in that scheme were not invited. Among the persons who promoted the calling of this council were William Webb, Martin R. Delaney, J. Gould Bias, Franklin Turner, Augustus Greene, James M. Whitfield, William Lambert, Henry Bibb, James T. Holly and Henry M. Collins.

There developed in this assembly three groups, one believing with Martin R. Delaney that it was best to go to the Niger Valley in Africa, another following the counsel of James M. Whitfield then interested in emigration to Central America, and a third supporting James T. Holly who insisted that Hayti offered the best opportunities for free persons of color desiring to leave the United States. Delaney was commissioned to proceed to Africa, where he succeeded in concluding treaties with eight

African kings who offered American Negroes inducements to settle in their respective countries. James Redpath, already interested in the scheme of colonization in Hayti, had preceded Holly there and with the latter as his coworker succeeded in sending to that country as many as two thousand emigrants, the first of whom sailed from this country in 1861. Owing to the lack of equipment adequate to the establishment of the settlement and the unfavorable climate, not more than one third of the emigrants remained. Some attention was directed to California and Central America just as in the case of Africa but nothing in that direction took tangible form immediately, and the Civil War following soon thereafter did not give some of these schemes a chance to materialize.

CHAPTER 5. THE SUCCESSFUL MIGRANT

The reader will naturally be interested in learning exactly what these thousands of Negroes did on free soil. To estimate these achievements the casual reader of contemporary testimony would now, as such persons did then, find it decidedly easy. He would say that in spite of the unfailing aid which philanthropists gave the blacks, they seldom kept themselves above want and, therefore, became a public charge, afflicting their communities with so much poverty, disease and crime that they were considered the lepers of society. The student of history, however, must look beyond these comments for the whole truth. One must take into consideration the fact that in most cases these Negroes escaped as fugitives without sufficient food and clothing to comfort them until they could reach free soil, lacking the small fund with which the pioneer usually provided himself in going to establish a home in the wilderness, and lacking, above all, initiative of which slavery had deprived them. Furthermore, these refugees with few exceptions had to go to places where they were not wanted and in some cases to points from which they were driven as undesirables, although preparation for their coming had sometimes gone to the extent of purchasing homes and making provision for employment upon arrival.

Several well-established Negro settlements in the North, moreover, were broken up by the slave hunters after the passing of the Fugitive Slave Law of 1850.

The increasing intensity of the hatred of the Negroes must be understood too both as a cause and result of their intolerable condition. Prior to 1800 the Negroes of the North were in fair circumstances. Until that time it was generally believed that the whites and the blacks would soon reach the advanced stage of living together on a basis of absolute equality. The Negroes had not at that time exceeded the number that could be assimilated by the sympathizing communities in that section. The intolerable legislation of the South, however, forced so many free Negroes in the rough to crowd northern cities during the first four decades of the nineteenth century that they could not be easily readjusted. The number seeking employment far exceeded the demand for labor and thus multiplied the number of vagrants and paupers, many of whom had already been forced to this condition by the Irish and Germans then immigrating into northern cities. At one time, as in the case of Philadelphia, the Negroes constituting a small fraction of the population furnished one half of the criminals. A radical opposition to the Negro followed, therefore, arousing first the laboring classes and finally alienating the support of the well-to-do people and the press. This condition obtained until 1840 in most northern communities and until 1850 in some places where the Negro population was considerable.

We must also take into account the critical labor situation during these years. The northern people were divided as to the way the Negroes should be encouraged. The mechanics of the North raised no objection to having the Negroes freed and enlightened but did not welcome them to that section as competitors in the struggle of life. When, therefore, the blacks, converted to the doctrine of training the hand to work with skill, began to appear in northern industrial centers there arose a formidable prejudice against them. Negro and white mechanics had once worked together but during the second quarter of the nineteenth century, when labor became more dignified and a larger number of white persons devoted themselves to skilled labor, they adopted the policy of eliminating the blacks. This opposition, to be sure, was not a mere harmless sentiment.

It tended to give rise to the organization of labor groups and finally to that of trades unions, the beginnings of those controlling this country today. Carrying the fight against the Negro still further, these laboring classes used their influence to obtain legislation against the employment of Negroes in certain pursuits.

Maryland and Georgia passed laws restricting the privileges of Negro mechanics, and Pennsylvania followed their example.

Even in those cases when the Negroes were not disturbed in their new homes on free soil, it was, with the exception of the Quaker and a few other communities, merely an act of toleration. It must not be concluded, however, that the Negroes then migrating to the North did not receive considerable aid. The fact to be noted here is that because they were not well received sometimes by the people of their new environment, the help which they obtained from friends afar off did not suffice to make up for the deficiency of community cooperation. This, of course, was an unusual handicap to the Negro, as his life as a slave tended to make him a dependent rather than a pioneer.

It is evident, however, from accessible statistics that wherever the Negro was adequately encouraged he succeeded. When the urban Negroes in northern communities had emerged from their crude state they easily learned from the white men their method of solving the problems of life. This tendency was apparent after 1840 and striking results of their efforts were noted long before the Civil War. They showed an inclination to work when positions could be found, purchased homes, acquired other property, built churches and established schools. Going even further than this, some of them, taking advantage of their opportunities in the business world, accumulated considerable fortunes, just as had been done in certain centers in the South where Negroes had been given a chance.

In cities far north like Boston not so much difference as to the result of this migration was noted. Some economic progress among the Negroes had early been observed there as a result of the long residence of Negroes in that city as in the case of Lewis Hayden who established a successful clothing business. In New York such evidences were more apparent. There were in that city not so many Negroes as frequented some other northern communities of this time but enough to make for that city a decidedly perplexing problem. It was the usual situation of ignorant, helpless fugitives and free Negroes going, they knew not where, to find a better country. The situation at times became so grave that it not only caused prejudice but gave rise to intense opposition against those who defended the cause of the blacks as in the case of the abolition riots which occurred at several places in the State in 1834.

To relieve this situation, Gerrit Smith, an unusually philanthropic gentleman, came forward with an interesting plan. Having large tracts of land in the southeastern counties of New York, he proposed to settle on small farms a large number of those Negroes huddled together in the congested districts of New York City. Desiring to obtain only the best class, he requested that the Negroes to be thus colonized be recommended by Reverend Charles B. Ray, Reverend Theodore S. Wright and Dr. J. McCune Smith, three Negroes of New York City, known to be representative of the best of the race. Upon their recommendations he deeded unconditionally to black men in 1846 three hundred small farms in Franklin, Essex, Hamilton, Fulton, Oneida, Delaware, Madison and Ulster counties, giving to each settler beside $10.00 to enable him to visit his farm. With these holdings the blacks would not only have a basis for economic independence but would have sufficient property to meet the special qualifications which New York by the law of 1823 required of Negroes offering to vote.

This experiment, however, was a failure. It was not successful because of the intractability of the land, the harshness of the climate, and, in a great measure, the inefficiency of the settlers. They had none of the qualities of farmers. Furthermore, having been disabled by infirmities and vices they could not as beneficiaries answer the call of the benefactor. Peterboro, the town opened to Negroes in this section, did maintain a school and served as a station of the Underground Railroad but the agricultural results expected of the enterprise never materialized. The main difficulty in this case was the impossibility of substituting something foreign for individual enterprise.

Progressive Negroes did appear, however, in other parts of the State. In Penyan, Western New York, William Platt and Joseph C. Cassey were successful lumber merchants. Mr. W.H. Topp of Albany was for several years one of the leading merchant tailors of that city. Henry Scott, of New York City, developed a successful pickling business, supplying most of the vessels entering that port. Thomas Downing for thirty years ran a creditable restaurant in the midst of the Wall Street banks, where he made a fortune.

Edward V. Clark conducted a thriving business, handling jewelry and silverware. The Negroes as a whole, moreover, had shown progress. Aided by the Government and philanthropic white people, they had before the Civil War a school system with primary, intermediate and grammar schools and a normal department. They then had considerable property, several churches and some benevolent institutions.

In Southern Pennsylvania, nearer to the border between the slave and free States, the effects of the achievements of these Negroes were more apparent for the reason that in these urban centers there were sufficient Negroes for one to be helpful to the other. Philadelphia presented then the most striking example of the remaking of these people. Here the handicap of the foreign element was greatest, especially after 1830. The Philadelphia Negro, moreover, was further impeded in his progress by the presence of southerners who made Philadelphia their home, and still more by the prejudice of those Philadelphia merchants who, sustaining such close relations to the South, hated the Negro and the abolitionists who antagonized their customers.

In spite of these untoward circumstances, however, the Negroes of Philadelphia achieved success. Negroes who had formerly been able to toil upward were still restricted but they had learned to make opportunities. In 1832 the Philadelphia blacks had $350,000 of taxable property, $359,626 in 1837 and $400,000 in 1847. These Negroes had 16 churches and 100 benevolent societies in 1837 and 19 churches and 106 benevolent societies in 1847. Philadelphia then had more successful Negro schools than any other city in the country. There were also about 500 Negro mechanics in spite of the opposition of organized labor. Some of these Negroes, of course, were natives of that city.

Chief among those who had accumulated considerable property was Mr. James Forten, the proprietor of one of the leading sail manufactories, constantly employing a large number of men, black and white. Joseph Casey, a broker of considerable acumen, also accumulated desirable property, worth probably $75,000. Crowded out of the higher pursuits of labor, certain other enterprising business men of this group organized the Guild of Caterers. This was composed of such men as Bogle, Prosser, Dorsey, Jones and Minton. The aim was to elevate the Negro waiter and cook from the plane of menials to that of progressive business men. Then came Stephen Smith who amassed a large fortune as a lumber merchant and with him Whipper, Vidal and Purnell. Still and Bowers were reliable coal merchants, Adger a success in handling furniture, Bowser a well-known painter, and William H. Riley the intelligent bootmaker.

There were a few such successful Negroes in other communities in the State. Mr. William Goodrich, of York, acquired considerable interest in the branch of the Baltimore and Ohio Railroad extending to Lancaster. Benjamin Richards, of Pittsburgh, amassed a large fortune running a butchering business, buying by contract droves of cattle to supply the various military posts of the United States. Mr. Henry M. Collins, who started life as a boatman, left this position for speculation in real estate in Pittsburgh where he established himself as an asset of the community and accumulated considerable wealth. Owen A. Barrett, of the same city, made his way by discovering the remedy known as B.A. Fahnestock's Celebrated Vermifuge, for which he was retained in the employ of the proprietor, who exploited the remedy. Mr. John Julius made himself indispensable to Pittsburgh by running the Concert Hall Cafe where he served President William Henry Harrison in 1840.

The field of greatest achievement, however, was not in the conservative East where the people had well established their going toward an enlightened and sympathetic aristocracy of talent and wealth. It was in the West where men were in position to establish themselves anew and make of life what they would. These crude communities, to be sure, often objected to the presence of the Negroes and sometimes drove them out. But, on the other hand, not a few of those centers in the making were in the hands of the Quakers and other philanthropic persons who gave the Negroes a chance to grow up with the community, when they exhibited a capacity which justified philanthropic efforts in their behalf.

These favorable conditions obtained especially in the towns along the Ohio river, where so many fugitives and free persons of color stopped on their way from slavery to freedom. In Steubenville a number of Negroes had by their industry and

maker.

There were a few such successful Negroes in other communities in the State. Mr. William Goodrich, of York, acquired considerable interest in the branch of the Baltimore and Ohio Railroad extending to Lancaster. Benjamin Richards, of Pittsburgh, amassed a large fortune running a butchering business, buying by contract droves of cattle to supply the various military posts of the United States. Mr. Henry M. Collins, who started life as a boatman, left this position for speculation in real estate in Pittsburgh where he established himself as an asset of the community and accumulated considerable wealth. Owen A. Barrett, of the same city, made his way by discovering the remedy known as B.A. Fahnestock's Celebrated Vermifuge, for which he was retained in the employ of the proprietor, who exploited the remedy. Mr. John Julius made himself indispensable to Pittsburgh by running the Concert Hall Cafe where he served President William Henry Harrison in 1840.

The field of greatest achievement, however, was not in the conservative East where the people had well established their going toward an enlightened and sympathetic aristocracy of talent and wealth. It was in the West where men were in position to establish themselves anew and make of life what they would. These crude communities, to be sure, often objected to the presence of the Negroes and sometimes drove them out. But, on the other hand, not a few of those centers in the making were in the hands of the Quakers and other philanthropic persons who gave the Negroes a chance to grow up with the community, when they exhibited a capacity which justified philanthropic efforts in their behalf.

These favorable conditions obtained especially in the towns along the Ohio river, where so many fugitives and free persons of color stopped on their way from slavery to freedom. In Steubenville a number of Negroes had by their industry and

the handicap of the foreign element was greatest, especially after 1830. The Philadelphia Negro, moreover, was further impeded in his progress by the presence of southerners who made Philadelphia their home, and still more by the prejudice of those Philadelphia merchants who, sustaining such close relations to the South, hated the Negro and the abolitionists who antagonized their customers.

In spite of these untoward circumstances, however, the Negroes of Philadelphia achieved success. Negroes who had formerly been able to toil upward were still restricted but they had learned to make opportunities. In 1832 the Philadelphia blacks had $350,000 of taxable property, $359,626 in 1837 and $400,000 in 1847. These Negroes had 16 churches and 100 benevolent societies in 1837 and 19 churches and 106 benevolent societies in 1847. Philadelphia then had more successful Negro schools than any other city in the country. There were also about 500 Negro mechanics in spite of the opposition of organized labor. Some of these Negroes, of course, were natives of that city.

Chief among those who had accumulated considerable property was Mr. James Forten, the proprietor of one of the leading sail manufactories, constantly employing a large number of men, black and white. Joseph Casey, a broker of considerable acumen, also accumulated desirable property, worth probably $75,000. Crowded out of the higher pursuits of labor, certain other enterprising business men of this group organized the Guild of Caterers. This was composed of such men as Bogle, Prosser, Dorsey, Jones and Minton. The aim was to elevate the Negro waiter and cook from the plane of menials to that of progressive business men. Then came Stephen Smith who amassed a large fortune as a lumber merchant and with him Whipper, Vidal and Purnell. Still and Bowers were reliable coal merchants, Adger a success in handling furniture, Bowser a well-known painter, and William H. Riley the intelligent boot-

good deportment made themselves helpful to the community. Stephen Mulber who had been in that town for thirty years was in 1835 the leader of a group of thrifty free persons of color. He had a brick dwelling, in which he lived, and other property in the city. He made his living as a master mechanic employing a force of workmen to meet the increasing demand for his labor. In Gallipolis, there was another group of this class of Negroes, who had permanently attached themselves to the town by the acquisition of property. They were then able not only to provide for their families but were maintaining also a school and a church. In Portsmouth, Ohio, despite the "Black Friday" upheaval of 1831, the Negroes settled down to the solution of the problems of their new environment and later showed in the accumulation of property evidences of actual progress. Among the successful Negroes in Columbus was David Jenkins who acquired considerable property as a painter, glazier and paper hanger. One Mr. Hill, of Chillicothe, was for several years its leading tanner and currier.

It was in Cincinnati, however, that the Negroes made most progress in the West. The migratory blacks came there at times in such large numbers, as we have observed, that they provoked the hostile classes of whites to employ rash measures to exterminate them. But the Negroes, accustomed to adversity, struggled on, endeavoring through schools and churches to embrace every opportunity to rise. By 1840 there were 2,255 Negroes in that city. They had, exclusive of personal effects and $19,000 worth of church property, accumulated $209,000 worth of real estate. A number of their progressive men had established a real estate firm known as the "Iron Chest" company which built houses for Negroes. One man, who had once thought it unwise to accumulate wealth from which he might be driven, had, by 1840, changed his mind and purchased $6,000 worth of real estate.

Another Negro paid $5,000 for himself and family and

bought a home worth

$800 or $1,000. A freedman, who was a slave until he was twenty-four years of age, then had two lots worth $10,000, paid a tax of $40 and had 320 acres of land in Mercer County. Another, who was worth only $3,000 in 1836, had seven houses in 1840, 400 acres of land in Indiana, and another tract in Mercer County, Ohio. He was worth altogether about $12,000 or $15,000. A woman who was a slave until she was thirty was then worth $2,000. She had also come into potential possession of two houses on which a white lawyer had given her a mortgage to secure the payment of $2,000 borrowed from this thrifty woman. Another Negro, who was on the auction block in 1832, had spent $2,600 purchasing himself and family and had bought two brick houses worth $6,000 and 560 acres of land in Mercer County, Ohio, said to be worth $2,500.

The Negroes of Cincinnati had as early as 1820 established schools which developed during the forties into something like a modern system with Gilmore's High School as a capstone. By that time they had also not only several churches but had given time and means to the organization and promotion of such as the Sabbath School Youth's Society, the Total

Abstinence Temperance Society and the Anti-Slavery Society. The worthy example set by the Negroes of this city was a stimulus to noble endeavor and significant achievements of Negroes throughout the Ohio and Mississippi Valleys. Disarming their enemies of the weapon that they would continue a public charge, they secured the cooperation of a larger number of white people who at first had treated them with contempt.

This unusual progress in the Ohio valley had been promoted by two forces, the development of the steamboat as

CHAPTER 6. CONFUSING MOVEMENTS

The Civil War waged largely in the South started the most exciting movement of the Negroes hitherto known. The invading Union forces drove the masters before them, leaving the slaves and sometimes poor whites to escape where they would or to remain in helpless condition to constitute a problem for the northern army. Many poor whites of the border States went with the Confederacy, not always because they wanted to enter the war, but to choose what they considered the lesser of two evils. The slaves soon realized a community of interests with the Union forces sent, as they thought, to deliver them from thralldom. At first, it was difficult to determine a fixed policy for dealing with these fugitives. To drive them away was an easy matter, but this did not solve the problem. General Butler's action at Fortress Monroe in 1861, however, anticipated the policy finally adopted by the Union forces. Hearing that three fugitive slaves who were received into his lines were to have been employed in building fortifications for the Confederate army, he declared them seized as contraband of war rather than declare them actually free as did General Fremont and General Hunter. He then gave them employment for wages and rations and appropriated to the support of the unemployed a portion of the earnings of the laborers. This policy was followed by General Wood, Butler's successor, and by General Banks in New Orleans.

An elaborate plan for handling such fugitives was carried out by E.S. Pierce and General Rufus Saxton at Port Royal, South Carolina. Seeing the situation in another light, however, General Halleck in charge in the West excluded slaves from the Union lines, at first, as did General Dix in Virginia. But Halleck, in his instructions to General McCullum, February, 1862, ordered him to put contrabands to work to pay for food and clothing. Other commanders, like General McCook and General Johnson, permitted the slave hunters to enter their lines and take their slaves upon identification, ignoring the confiscation act of August, 1861, which was construed by some as justifying the retention of such refugees. Officers of a different attitude, however, soon began to protest against the returning of fugitive slaves.

General Grant, also, while admitting the binding force of General Halleck's order, refused to grant permits to those in search of fugitives seeking asylum within his lines and at the capture of Fort Donelson ordered the retention of all blacks who had been used by the Confederates in building fortifications.

Lincoln finally urged the necessity for withholding fugitive slaves from the enemy, believing that there could be in it no danger of servile insurrection and that the Confederacy would thereby be weakened. As this opinion soon developed into a conviction that official action was necessary, Congress, by Act of March 13, 1862, provided that slaves be protected against the claims of their pursuers. Continuing further in this direction, the Federal Government gradually reached the position of withdrawing Negro labor from the Confederate territory. Finally the United States Government adopted the policy of withholding from the Confederates, slaves received with the understanding that their masters were in rebellion against the United States. With this as a settled policy then, the United States Government had to work out some scheme for the remaking of these fugitives coming into its camps.

In some of these cases the fugitives found themselves among men more hostile to them than their masters were, for many of the Union soldiers of the border States were slaveholders themselves and northern soldiers did not understand that they were fighting to free Negroes. The condition in which they were on arriving, moreover, was a new problem for the army. Some came naked, some in decrepitude, some afflicted with disease, and some wounded in their efforts to escape. There were "women in travail, the helplessness of childhood and of old age, the horrors of sickness and of frequent deaths." In their crude state few of them had any conception of the significance of liberty, thinking that it meant idleness and freedom from restraint. In consequence of this ignorance there developed such undesirable habits as deceit, theft and licentiousness to aggravate the afflictions of nakedness, famine and disease.

In the East large numbers of these refugees were concentrated at Washington, Alexandria, Fortress Monroe, Hampton, Craney Island and Fort Norfolk. There were smaller groups of them at Yorktown, Suffolk and Portsmouth.

[Illustration: MAP SHOWING THE PER CENT OF NEGROES IN TOTAL POPULATION, BY

STATES: 1910.

(Map 2, Bulletin 129, The United States Bureau of the Census.)]

Some of them were conducted from these camps into York, Columbia, Harrisburg, Pittsburgh and Philadelphia, and by water to New York and Boston, from which they went to various parts seeking labor. Some collected in groups as in the case of those at Five Points in New York. Large numbers of them from Virginia assembled in Washington in 1862 in Duff Green's Row on Capitol Hill where they were organized as a camp, out of which came a contraband school, after being moved to the McClellan Barracks. Then there was in the District of Columbia another group known as Freedmen's village on Arlington Heights. It was said that, in 1864, 30,000 to 40,000 Negroes had come from the plantations to the District of Columbia. It happened here too as in most cases of this migration that the Negroes were on hand before the officials grappling with many other problems could determine exactly what could or should be done with them. The camps near Washington fortunately became centers for the employment of contrabands in the city. Those repairing to Fortress Monroe were distributed as laborers among the farmers of that vicinity.

[Illustration: DIAGRAM SHOWING THE NEGRO POPULATION OF NORTHERN AND

WESTERN CITIES IN 1900 AND THE EXTENT TO WHICH IT INCREASED BY 1910.

COUNTIES IN THE SOUTHERN STATES HAVING AT LEAST 50 PER CENT OF THEIR POPULATION NEGRO.

(Maps 3 and 4, Bulletin 129, U.S. Bureau of the Census.) (Maps 5 and 6, Bulletin 129, U.S. Bureau of the Census.)]

In some of these camps, and especially in those of the West, the refugees were finally sent out to other sections in need of labor, as in the cases of the contrabands assembled with the Union army at first at Grand Junction and later at Memphis.

There were three types of these camp communities which attracted attention as places for free labor experimentation. These were at Port Royal, on the Mississippi in the neighborhood of Vicksburg, and in Lower Louisiana and Virginia. The first trial of free labor of blacks on a large scale in a slave State was made in Port Royal. The experiment was generally successful. By industry, thrift and orderly conduct the Negroes showed their appreciation for their new opportunities. In the Mississippi section invaded by the northern army, General

Thomas opened what he called Infirmary Farms which he leased to Negroes on certain terms which they usually met successfully. The same plan, however, was not so successful in the Lower Mississippi section. The failure in this section was doubtless due to the inferior type of blacks in the lower cotton belt where Negroes had been more brutalized by slavery.

In some cases, these refugees experienced many hardships. It was charged that they were worked hard, badly treated and deprived of all their wages except what was given them for rations and a scanty pittance, wholly insufficient to purchase necessary clothing and provide for their families.

Not a few of the refugees for these reasons applied for permission to return to their masters and sometimes such permission was granted; for, although under military authority, they were by order of Congress to be considered as freemen. These voluntary slaves, of course, were few and the authorities were not thereby impressed with the thought that Negroes would prefer to be slaves, should they be treated as freemen rather than as brutes.

It became increasingly difficult, however, to handle this problem. In the first place, it was not an easy matter to find soldiers well disposed to serve the Negroes in any manner whatever and the officers of the army had no desire to force them to render such services since those thus engaged suffered a sort of social ostracism. The same condition obtained in the case of caring for those afflicted with disease, until there was issued a specific regulation placing the contraband sick in charge of the army surgeons. What the situation in the Mississippi Valley was during these months has been well described by an observer, saying: "I hope I may never be called on again to witness the horrible scenes I saw in those first days of history of the freedmen in the Mississippi Valley. Assistants were hard to find, especially the kind that would do any good in the camps. A detailed soldier in each camp of a thousand people was the best that could be done and his duties were so onerous that he ended by doing nothing. In reviewing the condition of the people at that time, I am not surprised at the marvelous stories told by visitors who caught an occasional glimpse of the misery and wretchedness in these camps. Our efforts to do anything for these people, as they herded together in masses, when founded on any expectation that they would help themselves, often failed; they had become so completely broken down in spirit, through suffering, that it was almost impossible to arouse them."

A few sympathetic officers and especially the chaplains undertook to relieve the urgent cases of distress. They could do little, however, to handle all the problems of the unusual situation until they engaged the attention of the higher officers of the army and the federal functionaries in Washington.

After some delay this was finally done and special officers were detailed to take charge of the contrabands. The Negroes were assembled in camps and employed according to instructions from the Secretary of War as teamsters, laborers and the like on forts and railroads. Some were put to picking, ginning, baling and removing cotton on plantations abandoned by their masters. General Grant, as early as 1862, was making further use of them as fatigue men in the department of the surgeon-general, the quartermaster and the commissary. He believed then that such Negroes as did well in these more humble positions should be made citizens and soldiers. As a matter of fact out of this very suggestion came the policy of arming the Negroes, the first regiment of whom was recruited under orders issued by General Hunter at Port Royal, South Carolina in 1862. As the arming of the slave to participate in this war did not generally please the white people who considered the struggle a war between civilized groups, this policy could not offer general relief to the congested contraband camps.

A better system of handling the fugitives was finally worked out, however, with a general superintendent at the head of each department, supported by a number of competent assistants. More explicit instructions were given as to the manner of dealing with the situation. It was to be the duty of the superintendent of contrabands, says the order, to organize them into working parties in saving the cotton, as pioneers on railroads and steamboats, and in any way where their services could be made available.

Where labor was performed for private individuals they were charged in accordance with the orders of the commander of the department. In case they were directed to save abandoned crops of cotton for the benefit of the United States Government, the officer selling such crops would turn over to the superintendent of contrabands the proceeds of the sale, which together with other earnings were used for clothing and feeding the Negroes.

Clothing sent by philanthropic persons to these camps was received and distributed by the superintendent. In no case, however, were Negroes to be forced into the service of the United States Government or to be enticed away from their homes except when it became a military necessity.

Some order out of the chaos eventually developed, for as John Eaton, one of the workers in the West, reported: "There was no promiscuous intermingling. Families were established by themselves. Every man took care of his own wife and children." "One of the most touching features of our Work," says he, "was the eagerness with which colored men and women availed themselves of the opportunities offered them to legalize unions already formed, some of which had been in existence for a long time." "Chaplain A.S. Fiske on one occasion married in about an hour one hundred and nineteen couples at one service, chiefly those who had long lived together." Letters from the Virginia camps and from those of Port Royal indicate that this favorable condition generally obtained.

This unusual problem in spite of additional effort, however, would not readily admit of solution. Benevolent workers of the North, therefore, began to minister to the needs of these unfortunate blacks. They sent considerable sums of money, increasing quantities of clothing and even some of their most devoted men and women to toil among them as social workers and teachers. These efforts also took organized form in various parts of the North under the direction of The Pennsylvania Freedmen's Relief Association, The Tract Society, The American Missionary Association, Pennsylvania Friends Freedmen's Relief Association, Old School Presbyterian Mission, The Reformed Presbyterian Mission, The New England Freedmen's Aid Committee, The New England Freedmen's Aid Society, The New England Freedmen's Mission, The Washington Christian Union, The Universalists of Maine, The New York Freedmen's Relief Association, The Hartford Relief Society, The National Freedmen's Relief Association of the District of Columbia, and finally the Freedmen's Bureau.

As an outlet to the congested grouping of Negroes and poor whites in the war camps it was arranged to send a number of them to the loyal States as fast as there presented themselves opportunities for finding homes and employment. Cairo, Illinois, in the West, became the center of such activities extending its ramifications into all parts of the invaded southern territory.

Some of the refugees permanently settled in the North, taking up the work abandoned by the northern soldiers who went to war. It was soon found necessary to appoint a superintendent of such affairs at Cairo, for there were those who, desiring to lead a straggling life, had to be restrained from crime by military surveillance and regulations requiring labor for self-support. Exactly how many whites and blacks were thus aided to reach northern communities cannot be determined but in view of the frequent mention of their movements by travellers the number must have been considerable. In some cases, as in Lawrence, Kansas, there were assembled enough freedmen to constitute a distinct group. Speaking of this settlement the editor of the Alton Telegraph said in 1862 that although they amounted to many hundreds not one, that he could learn of, had been a public charge. They readily found employment at fair wages, and soon made themselves comfortable.

There was a little apprehension that the North would be overrun by such blacks. Some had no such fear, however, for the reason that the census did not indicate such a movement. Many slaves were freed in the North prior to 1860, yet with all the emigration from the slave States to the North there were then in all the Northern States but 226,152 free blacks, while there were in the slave States 261,918, an excess of 35,766 in the slave States.

Frederick Starr believed that during the Civil War there might be an influx for a few months but it would not continue. They would return when sure that they would be free. Starr thought that, if necessary, these refugees might be used in building the much desired Pacific Railroad to divert them from the North.

There was little ground for this apprehension, in fact, if their readjustment and development in the contraband camps could be considered an indication of what the Negroes would eventually do. Taking all things into consideration, most unbiased observers felt that blacks in the camps deserved well of their benefactors. According to Levi Coffin, these contrabands were, in 1864, disposed of as follows: "In military services as soldiers, laundresses, cooks, officers' servants and laborers in the various staff departments, 41,150; in cities, on plantations and in freedmen's villages and cared for, 72,500. Of these 62,300 were entirely self-supporting, just as any industrial class anywhere else, as planters, mechanics, barbers, hackmen and draymen, conducting enterprises on their own responsibility or working as hired laborers." The remaining 10,200 received subsistence from the government. 3,000 of these were members of families whose heads were carrying on plantations, and had undertaken cultivation of 4,000 acres of cotton, pledging themselves to pay the government for their subsistence from the first income of the crop. The other 7,200 included the paupers, that is, all Negroes over and under the self-supporting age, the crippled and sick in hospitals. This class, however, instead of being unproductive, had then under cultivation 500 acres of corn, 790 acres of vegetables, and 1,500 acres of cotton, besides working at wood chopping and other industries. There were reported in the aggregate over 100,000 acres of cotton under cultivation, 7,000 acres of which were leased and cultivated by blacks. Some Negroes were managing as many as 300 or 400 acres each. Statistics showing exactly how much the numbers of contrabands in the various branches of the service increased are wanting, but in view of the fact that the few thousand soldiers here given increased to about 200,000 before the close of the Civil War, the other numbers must have been considerable, if they all grew the least proportionately.

Much industry was shown among these refugees. Under this new system they acquired the idea of ownership, and of the security of wages and learned to see the fundamental difference between freedom and slavery. Some Yankees, however, seeing that they did less work than did laborers in the North, considered them lazy, but the lack of industry was customary in the South and a river should not be expected to rise higher than its source. One of their superintendents said that they worked well without being urged, that there was among them a public opinion against idleness, which answered for discipline, and that those put to work with soldiers labored longer and did the nicer parts. "In natural tact and the faculty of getting a livelihood," says the same writer, "the contrabands are inferior to the Yankees, but quite equal to the mass of southern population." The Negroes also showed capacity to organize labor and use capital in the promotion of enterprises. Many of them purchased land and cultivated it to great profit both to the community and to themselves. Others entered the service of the government as mechanics and contractors, from the employment of which some of them realized handsome incomes.

The more important development, however, was that of manhood. This was best observed in their growing consciousness of rights, and their readiness to defend them, even when encroached upon by members of the white race. They quickly learned to appreciate freedom and exhibited evidences of manhood in their desire for the comforts and conveniences of life. They readily purchased articles of furniture within their means, bringing their home equipment up to the standard of that of persons similarly circumstanced. The indisposition to labor was overcome "in a healthy nature by instinct and motives of superior forces, such as love of life, the desire to be clothed and fed, the sense of security derived from provision for the future, the feeling of self-respect, the love of family and children and the convictions of duty."

These enterprises, begun in doubt, soon ceased to be a bare hope or possibility. They became during the war a fruition and a consummation, in that they produced Negroes "who would work for a living and fight for freedom." They were, therefore, considered "adapted to civil society." They had "shown capacity for knowledge, for free industry, for subordination to law and discipline, for soldierly fortitude, for social and family relations, for religious culture and aspiration. These qualities," said the observer, "when stirred, and sustained by the incitements and rewards of a just society, and combining with the currents of our continental civilization, will, under the guidance of a benevolent Providence which forgets neither them nor us, make them a constantly progressive race; and secure them ever after from the calamity of another enslavement, and ourselves from the worst calamity of being their oppressors."

It is clear that these smaller numbers of Negroes under favorable conditions could be easily adjusted to a new environment. When, however, all Negroes were declared free there set in a confused migration which was much more of a problem. The first thing the Negro did after realizing that he was free was to roam over the country to put his freedom to a test. To do this, according to many writers, he frequently changed his name, residence, employment and wife, sometimes carrying with him from the plantation the fruits of his own labor. Many of them easily acquired a dog and a gun and were disposed to devote their time to the chase until the assistance in the form of mules and land expected from the government materialized. Their emancipation, therefore, was interpreted not only as freedom from slavery but from responsibility. Where they were going they did not know but the towns and cities became very attractive to them.

Speaking of this upheaval in Virginia, Eckenrode says that many of them roamed over the country without restraint. "Released from their accustomed bonds," says Hall, "and filled with a pleasing, if not vague, sense of uncontrolled freedom, they flocked to the cities with little hope of obtaining remunerative work. Wagon loads of them were brought in from the country by the soldiers and dumped down to shift for themselves." Referring to the proclamation of freedom, in Georgia, Thompson asserts that their most general and universal response was to pick up and leave the home place to go somewhere else, preferably to a town. "The lure of the city was strong to the blacks, appealing to their social natures, to their inherent love for a crowd." Davis maintains that thousands of the 70,000 Negroes in Florida crowded into the Federal military camps and into towns upon realizing that they were free. According to Ficklen, the exodus of the slaves from the neighboring plantations of Louisiana into Baton Rouge, Carrollton and New Orleans was so great as to strain the resources of the Federal authorities to support them. Ten thousand poured into New Orleans alone. Fleming records that upon leaving their homes the blacks collected in gangs at the cross roads, in the villages and towns, especially near the military posts. The towns were filled with crowds of blacks who left their homes with absolutely nothing, "thinking that the government would care for them, or more probably, not thinking at all."

The portrayal of these writers of this phase of Reconstruction history contains a general truth, but in some cases the picture is overdrawn. The student of history must bear in mind that practically all of our histories of that period are based altogether on the testimony of prejudiced whites and are written from their point of view. Some of these writers have aimed to exaggerate the vagrancy of the blacks to justify the radical procedure of the whites in dealing with it. The Negroes did wander about thoughtlessly, believing that this was the most effective way to enjoy their freedom. But nothing else could be expected from a class who had never felt anything but the heel of oppression. History shows that such vagrancy has always followed the immediate emancipation of a large number of slaves. Many Negroes who flocked to the towns and army camps, moreover, had like their masters and poor whites seen their homes broken up or destroyed by the invading Union armies. Whites who had never learned to work were also roaming and in some cases constituted marauding bands.

There was, moreover, an actual drain of laborers to the lower and more productive lands in Mississippi and Louisiana. This developed later into a more considerable movement toward the Southwest just after the Civil War, the exodus being from South Carolina, Georgia, Alabama and Mississippi to Louisiana, Arkansas and Texas. Here was the pioneering spirit, a going to the land of more economic opportunities. This slow movement continued from about 1865 to 1875, when the development of the numerous railway systems gave rise to land speculators who induced whites and blacks to go west and southwest. It was a migration of individuals, but it was reported that as many as 35,000 Negroes were then persuaded to leave South Carolina and Georgia for Arkansas and Texas.

The usual charge that the Negro is naturally migratory is not true. This impression is often received by persons who hear of the thousands of Negroes who move from one place to another from year to year because of the desire to improve their unhappy condition. In this there is no tendency to migrate but an urgent need to escape undesirable conditions. In fact, one of the American Negroes' greatest shortcomings is that they are not sufficiently pioneering. Statistics show that the whites have more inclination to move from State to State than the Negro. To prove this assertion, Professor William O. Scroggs has shown that, in 1910, 16.6 per cent of the Negroes had moved to some other State than that in which they were born, while during the same period 22.4 per cent of the whites had done the same.

The South, however, was not disposed to look at the vagrancy of the ex- slaves so philosophically. That section had been devastated by war and to rebuild these waste places reliable labor was necessary. Legislatures of the slave States, therefore, immediately after the close of the war, granted the Negro nominal freedom but enacted measures of vagrancy and labor so as to reduce the Negro again almost to the status of a slave. White magistrates were given wide discretion in adjudging Negroes vagrants. Negroes had to sign contracts to work. If without what was considered a just cause the Negro left the employ of a planter, the former could be arrested and forced to work and in some sections with ball and chain. If the employer did not care to take him back he could be hired out by the county or confined in jail. Mississippi, Louisiana and South Carolina had further drastic features. By local ordinance in Louisiana every Negro had to be in the service of some white person, and by special laws of South Carolina and Mississippi the Negro became subject to a master almost in the same sense in which he was prior to emancipation. These laws, of course, convinced the government of the United States that the South had not yet decided to let slavery go and for that reason military rule and Congressional Reconstruction followed. In this respect the South did itself a great injury, for many of the provisions of the black codes, especially the vagrancy laws, were unnecessary. Most Negroes soon realized that freedom did not mean relief from responsibility and they quickly settled down to work after a rather protracted and exciting holiday.

During the last year of and immediately after the Civil War there set in another movement, not of a large number of Negroes but of the intelligent class who had during years of residence in the North enjoyed such advantages of contact and education as to make them desirable and useful as leaders in the Reconstruction of the South and the remaking of the race. In their tirades against the Carpet-bag politicians who handled the Reconstruction situation so much to the dissatisfaction of the southern whites, historians often forget to mention also that a large number of the Negro leaders who participated in that drama were also natives or residents of Northern States.

Three motives impelled these blacks to go South. Some had found northern communities so hostile as to impede their progress, many wanted to rejoin relatives from whom they had been separated by their flight from the land of slavery, and others were moved by the spirit of adventure to enter a new field ripe with all sorts of opportunities. This movement, together with that of migration to large urban communities, largely accounts for the depopulation and the consequent decline of certain colored communities in the North after 1865.

Some of the Negroes who returned to the South became men of national prominence. William J. Simmons, who prior to the Civil War was carried from South Carolina to Pennsylvania, returned to do religious and educational work in Kentucky. Bishop James W. Hood, of the African Methodist Episcopal Zion Church, went from Connecticut to North Carolina to engage in similar work. Honorable R.T. Greener, the first Negro graduate of Harvard, went from Philadelphia to teach in the District of Columbia and later to be a professor in the University of South Carolina. F.L. Cardoza, educated at the University of Edinburgh, returned to South Carolina and became State Treasurer. R.B. Elliot, born in Boston and educated in England, settled in South Carolina from which he was sent to Congress.

John M. Langston was taken to Ohio and educated but came back to Virginia his native State from which he was elected to Congress. J.T. White left Indiana to enter politics in Arkansas, becoming State Senator and later commissioner of public works and internal improvements. Judge Mifflin Wister Gibbs, a native of Philadelphia, purposely settled in Arkansas where he served as city judge and Register of United States Land Office. T. Morris Chester, of Pittsburgh, finally made his way to Louisiana where he served with distinction as a lawyer and held the position of Brigadier-General in charge of the

Louisiana State Guards under the Kellogg government. Joseph Carter Corbin, who was taken from Virginia to be educated at Chillicothe, Ohio, went later to Arkansas where he served as chief clerk in the post office at Little Rock and later as State Superintendent of Schools. Pinckney Benton Stewart Pinchback, who moved north for education and opportunity, returned to enter politics in Louisiana, which honored him with several important positions among which was that of Acting Governor.

CHAPTER 7. THE EXODUS TO THE WEST

Having come through the halcyon days of the Reconstruction only to find themselves reduced almost to the status of slaves, many Negroes deserted the South for the promising west to grow up with the country. The immediate causes were doubtless political. Bulldozing, a rather vague term, covering all such crimes as political injustice and persecution, was the source of most complaint. The abridgment of the Negroes' rights had affected them as a great calamity. They had learned that voting is one of the highest privileges to be obtained in this life and they wanted to go where they might still exercise that privilege. That persecution was the main cause was disputed, however, as there were cases of Negroes migrating from parts where no such conditions obtained. Yet some of the whites giving their version of the situation admitted that violent methods had been used so to intimidate the Negroes as to compel them to vote according to the dictation of the whites. It was also learned that the bulldozers concerned in dethroning the non-taxpaying blacks were an impecunious and irresponsible group themselves, led by men of the wealthy class.

Coming to the defense of the whites, some said that much of the persecution with which the blacks were afflicted was due to the fear of Negro uprisings, the terror of the days of slavery. The whites, however, did practically nothing to remove the underlying causes. They did not encourage education and made no efforts to cure the Negroes of faults for which slavery itself was to be blamed and consequently could not get the confidence of the blacks. The races tended rather to drift apart. The Negroes lived in fear of reenslavement while the whites believed that the war between the North and South would soon be renewed. Some Negroes thinking likewise sought to go to the North to be among friends. The blacks, of course, had come so to regard southern whites as their enemies as to render impossible a voluntary division in politics.

Among the worst of all faults of the whites was their unwillingness to labor and their tendency to do mischief. As there were so many to live on the labor of the Negroes they were reduced to a state a little better than that of bondage. The master class was generally unfair to the blacks. No longer responsible for them as slaves, the planters endeavored after the war to get their labor for nothing. The Negroes themselves had no land, no mules, no presses nor cotton gins, and they could not acquire sufficient capital to obtain these things. They were made victims of fraud in signing contracts which they could not understand and had to suffer the consequent privations and want aggravated by robbery and murder by the Ku Klux Klan.

The murder of Negroes was common throughout the South and especially in Louisiana. In 1875, General Sheridan said that as many as 3,500 persons had been killed and wounded in that State, the great majority of whom being Negroes; that 1,884 were killed and wounded in 1868, and probably 1,200 between 1868 and 1875. Frightful massacres occurred in the parishes of Bossier, Catahoula, Saint Bernard, Grant and Orleans. As most of these murders were for political reasons, the offenders were regarded by their communities as heroes rather than as criminals. A massacre of Negroes began in the parish of St. Landry on the 28th of September and continued for three days, resulting in the death of from 300 to 400. Thirteen captives were taken from the jail and shot and as many as twenty-five dead bodies were found burned in the woods. There broke out in the parish of Bossier another three-day riot during which two hundred Negroes were massacred. More than forty blacks were killed in the parish of Caddo during the following month. In fact, the number of murders, maimings and whippings during these months aggregated over one thousand. The result was that the intelligent Negroes were either intimidated or killed so that the illiterate masses of Negro voters might be ordered to refrain from voting the Republican ticket to strengthen the Democrats or be subjected to starvation through the operation of the mischievous land tenure and credit system.

What was not done in 1868 to overthrow the Republican regime was accomplished by a renewed and extended use of such drastic measures throughout the South in 1876.

Certain whites maintained, however, that the unrest was due to the work of radical politicians at the North, who had sent their emissaries south to delude the Negroes into a fever of migration. Some said it was a scheme to force the nomination of a certain Republican candidate for President in 1880. Others laid it to the charge of the defeated white and black Republicans who had been thrown from power by the whites upon regaining control of the reconstructed States. A few insisted that a speech delivered by Senator Windom in 1879 had given stimulus to the migration. Many southerners said that speculators in Kansas had adopted this plan to increase the value of their land. Then there were other theories as to the fundamental causes, each consisting of a charge of one political faction that some other had given rise to the movement, varying according as they were Bourbons, conservatives, native white Republicans, carpet-bag Republicans, or black Republicans.

Impartial observers, however, were satisfied that the movement was spontaneous to the extent that the blacks were ready and willing to go. Probably no more inducement was offered them than to other citizens among whom land companies sent agents to distribute literature. But the fundamental causes of the unrest were economic, for since the Civil War race troubles have never been sufficient to set in motion a large number of Negroes. The discontent resulted from the land-tenure and credit systems, which had restored slavery in a modified form.

After the Civil War a few Negroes in those parts, where such opportunities were possible, invested in real estate offered for sale by the impoverished and ruined planters of the conquered commonwealths. When, however, the Negroes lost their political power, their property was seized on the plea for delinquent taxes and they were forced into the ghetto of towns and cities, as it became a crime punishable by social proscription to sell Negroes desirable residences. The aim was to debase all Negroes to the status of menial labor in conformity with the usual contention of the South that slavery is the normal condition of the blacks.

Most of the land of the South, however, always remained as large tracts held by the planters of cotton, who never thought of alienating it to the Negroes to make them a race of small farmers. In fact, they had not the means to make extensive purchases of land, even if the planters had been disposed to transfer it. Still subject to the experimentation of white men, the Negroes accepted the plan of paying them wages; but this failed in all parts except in the sugar district, where the blacks remained contented save when disturbed by political movements. They then tried all systems of working on shares in the cotton districts; but this was finally abandoned because the planters in some cases were not able to advance the Negro tenant supplies, pending the growth of the crop, and some found the Negro too indifferent and lazy to make the partnership desirable. Then came the renting system which during the Reconstruction period was general in the cotton districts. This system threw the tenant on his own responsibility and frequently made him the victim of his own ignorance and the rapacity of the white man. As exorbitant prices were charged for rent, usually six to ten dollars an acre for land worth fifteen to thirty dollars an acre, the Negro tenant not only did not accumulate anything but had reason to rejoice at the end of the year, if he found himself out of debt.

Along with this went the credit system which furnished the capstone of the economic structure so harmful to the Negro tenant. This system made the Negroes dependent for their living on an advance of supplies of food, clothing or tools during the year, secured by a lien on the crop when harvested. As the Negroes had no chance to learn business methods during the days of slavery, they fell a prey to a class of loan sharks, harpies and vampires, who established stores everywhere to extort from these ignorant tenants by the mischievous credit system their whole income before their crops could be gathered. Some planters who sympathized with the Negroes brought forward the scheme of protecting them by advancing certain necessities at more reasonable prices. As the planter himself, however, was subject to usury, the scheme did not give much relief. The Negroes' crop, therefore, when gathered went either to the merchant or to the planter to pay the rent; for the merchant's supplies were secured by a mortgage on the tenant's personal property and a pledge of the growing crop. This often prevented Negro laborers in the employ of black tenants from getting their wages at the end of the year, for, although the laborer had also a lien on the growing crop, the merchant and the planter usually had theirs recorded first and secured thereby the support of the law to force the payment of their claims. The Negro tenant then began the year with three mortgages, covering all he owned, his labor for the coming year and all he expected to acquire during that twelvemonth. He paid "one-third of his product for the use of the land, he paid an exorbitant fee for recording the contract by which he paid his pound of flesh; he was charged two or three times as much as he ought to pay for ginning his cotton; and, finally, he turned over his crop to be eaten up in commissions, if any was still left to him."

The worst of all results from this iniquitous system was its effect on the Negroes themselves. It made the Negroes extravagant and unscrupulous. Convinced that no share of their crop would come to them when harvested, they did not exert themselves to produce what they could. They often abandoned their crops before harvest, knowing that they had already spent them. In cases, however, where the Negro tenants had acquired mules, horses or tools upon which the speculator had a mortgage, the blacks were actually bound to their landlords to secure the property. It was soon evident that in the end the white man himself was the loser by this evil system.

There appeared waste places in the country. Improvements were wanting, land lay idle for lack of sufficient labor, and that which was cultivated yielded a diminishing return on account of the ignorance and improvidence of those tilling it. These Negroes as a rule had lost the ambition to become landowners, preferring to invest their surplus money in personal effects; and in the few cases where the Negroes were induced to undertake the buying of land, they often tired of the responsibility and gave it up.

There began in the spring of 1879, therefore, an emigration of the Negroes from Louisiana and Mississippi to Kansas. For some time there was a stampede from several river parishes in Louisiana and from counties just opposite them in Mississippi. It was estimated that from five to ten thousand left their homes before the movement could be checked. Persons of influence soon busied themselves in showing the blacks the necessity for remaining in the South and those who had not then gone or prepared to go were persuaded to return to the plantations. This lull in the excitement, however, was merely temporary, for many Negroes had merely returned home to make more extensive preparations for leaving the following spring. The movement was accelerated by the work of two Negro leaders of some note, Moses Singleton, of Tennessee, the self-styled Moses of the Exodus; and Henry Adams, of Louisiana, who credited himself with having organized for this purpose as many as 98,000 blacks.

Taking this movement seriously a convention of the leading whites and blacks was held at Vicksburg, Mississippi, on the sixth of May, 1879. This body was controlled mainly by unsympathetic but diplomatic whites.

General N.R. Miles, of Yazoo County, Mississippi, was elected president and

A.W. Crandall, of Louisiana, secretary. After making some meaningless but eloquent speeches the convention appointed a committee on credentials and adjourned until the following day. On reassembling Colonel W.L. Nugent, chairman of the committee, presented a certain preamble and resolutions citing causes of the exodus and suggesting remedies. Among the causes, thought he, were: "the low price of cotton and the partial failure of the crop, the irrational system of planting adopted in some sections whereby labor was deprived of intelligence to direct it and the presence of economy to make it profitable, the vicious system of credit fostered by laws permitting laborers and tenants to mortgage crops before they were grown or even planted; the apprehension on the part of many colored people produced by insidious reports circulated among them that their civil and political rights were endangered or were likely to be; the hurtful and false rumors diligently disseminated, that by emigrating to Kansas the Negroes would obtain lands, mules and money from the government without cost to themselves, and become independent forever."

Referring to the grievances and proposing a redress, the committee admitted that errors had been committed by the whites and blacks alike, as each in turn had controlled the government of the States there represented. The committee believed that the interests of planters and laborers, landlords and tenants were identical; that they must prosper or suffer together; and that it was the duty of the planters and landlords of the State there represented to devise and adopt some contract by which both parties would receive the full benefit of labor governed by intelligence and economy. The convention affirmed that the Negro race had been placed by the constitution of the United States and the States there represented, and the laws thereof, on a plane of absolute equality with the white race; and declared that the Negro race should be accorded the practical enjoyment of all civil and political rights guaranteed by the said constitutions and laws.

The convention pledged itself to use whatever of power and influence it possessed to protect the Negro race against all dangers in respect to the fair expression of their wills at the polls, which they apprehended might result from fraud, intimidation or bulldozing on the part of the whites. And as there could be no liberty of action without freedom of thought, they demanded that all elections should be fair and free and that no repressive measures should be employed by the Negroes "to deprive their own race in part of the fullest freedom in the exercise of the highest right of citizenship."

The committee then recommended the abolition of the mischievous credit system, called upon the Negroes to contradict false reports as to crimes of the whites against them and, after considering the Negroes' right to emigrate, urged that they proceed about it with reason. Ex-Governor Foote, of Mississippi, submitted a plan to establish in every county a committee, composed of men who had the confidence of both whites and blacks, to be auxiliary to the public authorities, to listen to complaints and arbitrate, advise, conciliate or prosecute, as each case should demand. But unwilling to do more than make temporary concessions, the majority rejected Foote's plan.

The whites thought also to stop the exodus by inducing the steamboat lines not to furnish the emigrants' transportation. Negroes were also detained by writs obtained by preferring against them false charges. Some, who were willing to let the Negroes go, thought of importing white and Chinese labor to take their places. Hearing of the movement and thinking that he could offer a remedy, Senator D.W. Voorhees, of Indiana, introduced a resolution in the United States Senate authorizing an inquiry into the causes of the exodus. The movement, however, could not be stopped and it became so widespread that the people in general were forced to give it serious thought. Men in favor of it declared their views, organized migration societies and appointed agents to promote the enterprise of removing the freedmen from the South.

Becoming a national measure, therefore, the migration evoked expressions from Frederick Douglass and Richard T. Greener, two of the most prominent Negroes in the United States. Douglass believed that the exodus was ill- timed. He saw in it the abandonment of the great principle of protection to persons and property in every State of the Union. He felt that if the Negroes could not be protected in every State, the Federal Government was shorn of its rightful dignity and power, the late rebellion had triumphed, the sovereign of the nation was an empty vessel, and the power and authority in individual States were supreme. He thought, therefore, that it was better for the Negroes to stay in the South than to go North, as the South was a better market for the black man's labor. Douglass believed that the Negroes should be warned against a nomadic life. He did not see any more benefit in the migration to Kansas than he had years before in the emigration to Africa.

The Negroes had a monopoly of labor at the South and they would be too insignificant in numbers to have such an advantage in the North. The blacks were then potentially able to elect members of Congress in the South but could not hope to exercise such power in other parts. Douglass believed, moreover, that this exodus did not conform to the "laws of civilizing migration," as the carrying of a language, literature and the like of a superior race to an inferior; and it did not conform to the geographic laws assuring healthy migration from east to west in the same latitude, as this was from south to north, far away from the climate in which the migrants were born.

The exodus of the Negroes, however, was heartily endorsed by Richard T. Greener. He did not consider it the best remedy for the lawlessness of the South but felt that it was a salutary one. He did not expect the United States to give the oppressed blacks in the South the protection they needed, as there is no abstract limit to the right of a State to do anything. He would not encourage the Negro to lead a wandering life but in that instance such advice was gratuitous. Greener failed to find any analogy between African colonization and migration to the West as the former was promoted by slaveholders to remove the free Negro from the country and the other sprang spontaneously from the class considering itself aggrieved. "One led out of the country to a comparative wilderness; the other directed to a better land and larger opportunities." He did not see how the migration to the North would diminish the potentiality of the Negro in politics, for Massachusetts first elected Negroes to her General Court, Ohio had nominated a Negro representative and Illinois another. He showed also that Mr. Douglass's objection on the grounds of migrating from south to north rather than from east to west was not historical. He thought little of the advice to the Negroes to stick and fight it out, for he had evidence that the return of the unreconstructed Confederates to power in the South would for generations doom the blacks to political oppression unknown in the annals of a free country.

Greener showed foresight here in urging the Negroes to take up desirable western land before it would be preempted by foreigners. As the Swedes, Norwegians, Irish, Hebrews and others were organizing societies and raising funds to promote the migration of their needy to these lands, why should the Negroes be debarred? Greener had no apprehension as to the treatment the Negroes would receive in the West. He connected the movement too with the general welfare of the blacks, considering it a promising sign that they had learned to run from persecution. Having passed their first stage, that of appealing to philanthropists, the Negroes were then appealing to themselves.

Feeling very much as Greener did, these Negroes rushed into Kansas and neighboring States in 1879. So many came that some systematic relief had to be offered. Mrs. Comstock, a Quaker lady, organized for this purpose the Kansas Freedmen's Relief Association, to raise funds and secure for them food and clothing. In this work she had the support of Governor J.P. Saint John. There was much suffering upon arriving in Kansas but relief came from various sources. During this year $40,000 and 500,000 pounds of clothing, bedding and the like were used. England contributed 50,000 pounds of goods and $8,000. In 1879, the refugees took up 20,000 acres of land and brought 3,000 under cultivation. The Relief Association at first furnished them with supplies, teams and seed, which they profitably used in the production of large crops. Desiring to establish homes, they built 300 cabins and saved $30,000 the first year. In April, 1,300 refugees had gathered around Wyandotte alone. Up to that date 60,000 had come to Kansas, nearly 40,000 of whom arrived in destitute condition. About 30,000 settled in the country, some on rented lands and others on farms as laborers, leaving about 25,000 in cities, where on account of crowded conditions and the hard weather many greatly suffered. Upon finding employment, however, they all did well, most of them becoming self-supporting within one year after their arrival, and few of them coming back to the Relief Association for aid the second time. This was especially true of those in Topeka, Parsons and Kansas City.

The people of Kansas did not encourage the blacks to come. They even sent messengers to the South to advise the Negroes not to migrate and, if they did come anyway, to provide themselves with equipment. When they did arrive, however, they welcomed and assisted them as human beings. Under such conditions the blacks established five or six important colonies in Kansas alone between 1879 and 1880. Chief among these were Baxter Springs, Nicodemus, Morton City and Singleton. Governor Saint John, of Kansas, reported that they seemed to be honest and of good habits, were certainly industrious and anxious to work, and so far as they had been tried had proved to be faithful and excellent laborers. Giving his observations there, Sir George Campbell bore testimony to the same report. Out of these communities have come some most progressive black citizens. In consideration of their desirability their white neighbors have given them their cooperation, secured to them the advantages of democratic education, and honored a few of them with some of the most important positions in the State.

Although the greater number of these blacks went to Kansas, about 5,000 of them sought refuge in other Western States. During these years, Negroes gradually invaded Indian Territory and increased the number already infiltrated into and assimilated by the Indian nations. When assured of their friendly attitude toward the Indians, the Negroes were accepted by them as equals, even during the days of slavery when the blacks on account of the cruelties of their masters escaped to the wilderness. Here we are at sea as to the extent to which this invasion and subsequent miscegenation of the black and red races extended for the reason that neither the Indians nor these migrating Negroes kept records and the United States

Government has been disposed to classify all mixed breeds in tribes as Indians. Having equal opportunity among the red men, the Negroes easily succeeded. A traveler in Indian Territory in 1880 found their condition unusually favorable. The cosy homes and promising fields of these freedmen attracted his attention as striking evidences of their thrift. He saw new fences, additions to cabins, new barns, churches and school-houses indicating prosperity.

Given every privilege which the Indians themselves enjoyed, the Negroes could not be other than contented.

It was very unfortunate, however, that in 1889, when by proclamation of President Harrison the Oklahoma Territory was thrown open, the intense race prejudice of the white immigrants and the rule of the mob prevented a larger number of Negroes from settling in that promising commonwealth. Long since extensively advertised as valuable, the land of Oklahoma had become a coveted prize for the adventurous squatters invading the territory in defiance of the law before it was declared open for settlement. The rush came with all the excitement of pioneer days redoubled. Stakes were set, parcels of land were claimed, cabins were constructed in an hour and towns grew up in a day. Then came conflicting claims as to titles and rights of preemption culminating in fighting and bloodshed. And worst of all, with this disorderly group there developed the fixed policy of eliminating the Negroes entirely.

The Negro, however, was not entirely excluded. Some had already come into the territory and others in spite of the barriers set up continued to come. With the cooperation of the Indians, with whom they easily amalgamated they readjusted themselves and acquired sufficient wealth to rise in the economic world. Although not generally fortunate, a number of them have coal and oil lands from which they obtain handsome incomes and a few, like Sara Rector, have actually become rich. Dishonest white men with the assistance of unprincipled officials have defrauded and are still endeavoring to defraud these Negroes of their property, lending them money secured by mortgages and obtaining for themselves through the courts appointments as the Negroes' guardians. They turn out to be the robbers of the Negroes, in case they do not live in a community where an enlightened public opinion frowns down upon this crime.

During the later eighties and the early nineties there were some other interstate movements worthy of notice here. The mineral wealth of the Appalachian mountains was being exploited. Foreigners, at first, were coming into this country in sufficiently large numbers to meet the demand; but when this supply became inadequate, labor agents appealed to the blacks in the South. Negroes then flocked to the mining districts of Birmingham, Alabama, and to East Tennessee. A large number also migrated from North Carolina and Virginia to West Virginia and some few of the same group to Southern Ohio to take the places of those unreasonable strikers who often demanded larger increases in wages than the income of their employers could permit. Many of these Negroes came to West Virginia as is evidenced by the increase in Negro population of that State. West Virginia had a Negro population of 17,980 in 1870; 25,886 in 1880; 32,690 in 1890;

43,499 in 1900; and 64,173 in 1910.

CHAPTER 8. THE MIGRATION OF THE TALENTED TENTH

In spite of these interstate movements, the Negro still continued as a perplexing problem, for the country was unprepared to grant the race political and civil rights. Nominal equality was forced on the South at the point of the sword and the North reluctantly removed most of its barriers against the blacks. Some, still thinking, however, that the two races could not live together as equals, advocated ceding the blacks the region on the Gulf of Mexico. This was branded as chimerical on the ground that, deprived of the guidance of the whites, these States would soon sink to African level and the end of the experiment would be a reconquest and a military regime fatal to the true development of American institutions. Another plan proposed was the revival of the old colonization idea of sending Negroes to Africa, but this exhibited still less wisdom than the first in that it was based on the hypothesis of deporting a nation, an expense which no government would be willing to incur. There were then no physical means of transporting six or seven millions of people, moreover, as there would be a new born for every one the agents of colonization could deport.

With the deportation scheme still kept before the people by the American Colonization Society, the idea of emigration to Africa did not easily die.

Some Negroes continued to emigrate to Liberia from year to year. This policy was also favored by radicals like Senator Morgan, of Alabama, who, after movements like the Ku Klux Klan had done their work of intimidating Negroes into submission to the domination of the whites, concluded that most of the race believed that there was no future for the blacks in the United States and that they were willing to emigrate. These radicals advocated the deportation of the blacks to prevent the recurrence of "Negro domination." This plan was acceptable to the whites in general also, for, unlike the consensus of opinion of today, it was then thought that the South could get along without the Negro. Even newspapers like the Charleston News and Courier, which denounced the persecution of the Negroes, urged them to emigrate to Africa as they could not be permitted to rule over the white people. The Minneapolis Times wished the scheme success and Godspeed and believed that the sooner it was carried out the better it would be for the Negroes.

Most of the influential newspapers of the country, however, urged the contrary. Citing the progress of the Negroes since emancipation to show that the blacks were doing their full share toward developing the wealth of the South, the Indianapolis Journal characterized as barbarism the suggestion that the government should furnish them transportation to Africa. "The ancestors of most of the Negroes now in this country," said the editor, "have doubtless been here as long as those of Senator Morgan, and their descendants are as thoroughly acclimated and have as good a right here as the Senator himself." This was the opinion of all useful Negroes except Bishop H.M. Turner, who endorsed Morgan's plan by advocating the emigration of one fourth of the blacks to Africa. The editor of the Chicago Record-Herald entreated Turner to temper his enthusiasm with discretion before he involved in unspeakable disaster any more of his trustful compatriots.

Speaking more plainly to the point, the editor of the Philadelphia North American said that the true interest of the South was to accommodate itself to changed conditions and that the duty of the freedmen lies in making themselves worth more in the development of the South than they were as chattels. Although recognizing the disabilities and hardships of the South both to the whites and the blacks, he could not believe that the elimination of the Negroes would, if practicable, give relief. The Boston Herald inquired whether it was worth while to send away a laboring population in the absence of whites to take its place and referred to the misfortunes of Spain which undertook to carry out such a scheme. Speaking the real truth, The Milwaukee Journal said that no one needed to expect any appreciable decrease in the black population through any possible emigration, no matter how successful it might be. "The Negro," said the editor, "is here to stay and our institutions must be adapted to comprehend him and develop his possibilities." The Colored American, then the leading Negro organ of thought in the United States, believed that the Negroes should be thankful to Senator Morgan for his attitude on emigration, because he might succeed in deporting to Africa those Negroes who affect to believe that this is not their home and the more quickly we get rid of such foolhardy people the better it will be for the stalwart of the race.

A number of Negroes, however, under the inspiration of leaders like Bishop

H.M. Turner, did not feel that the race had a fair chance in the United States. A few of them emigrated to Wapimo, Mexico; but, becoming dissatisfied with the situation there, they returned to their homes in Georgia and Alabama in 1895. The coming of the Negroes into Mexico caused suspicion and excitement. A newspaper, El Tiempo, which had been denouncing lynching in the United States, changed front when these Negroes arrived in that country.

Going in quest of new opportunities and desiring to reenforce the civilization of Liberia, 197 other Negroes sailed from Savannah, Georgia, for Liberia, March 19, 1895. Commending this step, the Macon

Telegraph referred to their action as a rebellion against the social laws which govern all people of this country. This organ further said that it was the outcome of a feeling which has grown stronger and stronger year by year among the Negroes of the Southern States and which will continue to grow with the increase of education and intelligence among them. The editor conceded that they had an opportunity to better their material condition and acquire wealth here but contended that they had no chance to rise out of the peasant class. The Memphis Commercial Appeal urged the building of a large Negro nation in Africa as practicable and desirable, for it was "more and more apparent that the Negro in this country must remain an alien and a disturber," because there was "not and can never be a future for him in this country." The Florida Times Union felt that this colonization scheme, like all others, was a fraud. It referred to the Negro's being carried to the land of plenty only to find out that there, as everywhere else in the world, an existence must be earned by toil and that his own old sunny southern home is vastly the better place.

Only a few intelligent Negroes, however, had reached the position of being contented in the South. The Negroes eliminated from politics could not easily bring themselves around to thinking that they should remain there in a state of recognized inferiority, especially when during the eighties and nineties there were many evidences that economic as well as political conditions would become worse. The exodus treated in the previous chapter was productive of better treatment for the Negroes and an increase in their wages in certain parts of the South but the migration, contrary to the expectations of many, did not become general. Actual prosperity was impossible even if the whites had been willing to give the Negro peasants a fair chance. The South had passed through a disastrous war, the effects of which so blighted the hopes of its citizens in the economic world that their land seemed to pass, so to speak, through a dark age. There was then little to give the man far down when the one to whom he of necessity looked for employment was in his turn bled by the merchant or the banker of the larger cities, to whom he had to go for extensive credits.

Southern planters as a class, however, had not much sympathy for the blacks who had once been their property and the tendency to cheat them continued, despite the fact that many farmers in the course of time extricated themselves from the clutches of the loan sharks. There were a few Negroes who, thanks to the honesty of certain southern gentlemen, succeeded in acquiring considerable property in spite of their handicaps. They yielded to the white man's control in politics, when it seemed that it meant either to abandon that field or die, and devoted themselves to the accumulation of wealth and the acquisition of education.

This concession, however, did not satisfy the radical whites, as they thought that the Negro might some day return to power. Unfortunately, therefore, after the restoration of the control of the State governments to the master class, there swept over these commonwealths a wave of hostile legislation demanded by the poor white uplanders determined to debase the blacks to the status of the free Negroes prior to the Civil War. The Negroes have, therefore, been disfranchised in most reconstructed States, deprived of the privilege of serving in the State militia, segregated in public conveyances, and excluded from public places of entertainment. They have, moreover, been branded by public opinion as pariahs of society to be used for exploitation but not to be encouraged to expect that their status can ever be changed so as to destroy the barriers between the races in their social and political relations.

This period has been marked also by an effort to establish in the South a system of peonage not unlike that of Mexico, a sort of involuntary servitude in that one is considered legally bound to serve his master until a debt contracted is paid.

Such laws have been enacted in Florida, Alabama, Georgia, Mississippi, North Carolina and South Carolina. No such distinction in law has been able to stand the constitutional test of the United States courts as was evidenced by the decision of the Supreme Court in 1911 declaring the Alabama law unconstitutional. But the planters of the South, still a law unto themselves, have maintained actual slavery in sequestered; districts where public opinion against peonage is too weak to support federal authorities in exterminating it. The Negroes themselves dare not protest under penalty of persecution and the peon concerned usually accepts his lot like that of a slave. Some years ago it was commonly reported that in trying to escape, the persons undertaking it often fail and suffer death at the hands of the planter or of murderous mobs, giving as their excuse, if any be required, that the Negro is a desperado or some other sort of criminal.

Unfortunately this reaction extended also to education. Appropriations to public schools for Negroes diminished from year to year and when there appeared practical leaders with, their sane plan for industrial education the South ignorantly accepted this scheme as a desirable subterfuge for seeming to support Negro education and at the same time directing the development of the blacks in such a way that they would never become the competitors of the white people. This was not these educators' idea but the South so understood it and in effecting the readjustment, practically left the Negroes out of the pale of the public school systems. Consequently, there has been added to the Negroes' misfortunes, in the South, that of being unable to obtain liberal education at public expense, although they themselves, as the largest consumers in some parts, pay most of the taxes appropriated to the support of schools for the youth of the other race.

The South, moreover, has adopted the policy of a more general intimidation of the Negroes to keep them down. The lynching of the blacks, at first for assaults on white women and later for almost any offense, has rapidly developed as an institution. Within the past fifty years there have been lynched in the South about 4,000 Negroes, many of whom have been publicly burned in the daytime to attract crowds that usually enjoy such feats as the tourney of the Middle Ages. Negroes who have the courage to protest against this barbarism have too often been subjected to indignities and in some cases forced to leave their communities or suffer the fate of those in behalf of whom they speak. These crimes of white men were at first kept secret but during the last two generations the culprits have become known as heroes, so popular has it been to murder Negroes. It has often been discovered also that the officers of these communities take part in these crimes and the worst of all is that politicians like Tillman, Blease and Vardaman glory in recounting the noble deeds of those who deserve so well of their countrymen for making the soil red with the Negroes' blood rather than permit the much feared Africanization of southern institutions.

In this harassing situation the Negro has hoped that the North would interfere in his behalf, but, with the reactionary Supreme Court of the United States interpreting this hostile legislation as constitutional in conformity with the demands of prejudiced public opinion, and with the leaders of the North inclined to take the view that after all the factions in the South must be left alone to fight it out, there has been nothing to be expected from without. Matters too have been rendered much worse because the leaders of the very party recently abandoning the freedmen to their fate, aggravated the critical situation by first setting the Negroes against their former masters, whom they were taught to regard as their worst enemies whether they were or not.

The last humiliation the Negroes have been forced to submit to is that of segregation. Here the effort has been to establish a ghetto in cities and to assign certain parts of the country to Negroes engaged in farming. It always happens, of course, that the best portion goes to the whites and the least desirable to the blacks, although the promoters of the segregation maintain that both races are to be treated equally. The ultimate aim is to prevent the Negroes of means from figuring conspicuously in aristocratic districts where they may be brought into rather close contact with the whites. Negroes see in segregation a settled policy to keep them down, no matter what they do to elevate themselves. The southern white man, eternally dreading the miscegenation of the races, makes the life, liberty and happiness of individuals second to measures considered necessary to prevent this so- called evil that this enviable civilization, distinctly American, may not be destroyed. The United States Supreme Court in the decision of the Louisville segregation case recently declared these segregation measures unconstitutional.

These restrictions have made the progress of the Negroes more of a problem in that directed toward social distinction, the Negroes have been denied the helpful contact of the sympathetic whites. The increasing race prejudice forces the whites to restrict their open dealing with the blacks to matters of service and business, maintaining even then the bearing of one in a sphere which the Negroes must not penetrate. The whites, therefore, never seeing the blacks as they are, and the blacks never being able to learn what the whites know, are thrown back on their own initiative, which their life as slaves could not have permitted to develop. It makes little difference that the Negroes have been free a few decades. Such freedom has in some parts been tantamount to slavery, and so far as contact with the superior class is concerned, no better than that condition; for under the old regime certain slaves did learn much by close association with their masters.

For these reasons there has been since the exodus to the

West a steady migration of Negroes from the South to points in the North. But this migration, mainly due to political changes, has never assumed such large proportions as in the case of the more significant movements due to economic causes, for, as the accompanying map shows, most Negroes are still in the South. When we consider the various classes migrating, however, it will be apparent that to understand the exodus of the Negroes to the North, this longer drawn out and smaller movement must be carefully studied in all its ramifications. It should be noted that unlike some of the other migrations it has not been directed to any particular State. It has been from almost all Southern States to various parts of the North and especially to the largest cities.

What classes then have migrated? In the first place, the Negro politicians, who, after the restoration of Bourbon rule in the South, found themselves thrown out of office and often humiliated and impoverished, had to find some way out of the difficulty. Some few have been relieved by sympathetic leaders of the Republican party, who secured for them federal appointments in Washington. These appointments when sometimes paying lucrative salaries have been given as a reward to those Negroes who, although dethroned in the South, remain in touch with the remnant of the Republican party there and control the delegates to the national conventions nominating candidates for President. Many Negroes of this class have settled in Washington. In some cases, the observer witnesses the pitiable scene of a man once a prominent public functionary in the South now serving in Washington as a messenger or a clerk.

The well-established blacks, however, have not been so easily induced to go. The Negroes in business in the South have usually been loath to leave their people among whom they can acquire property, whereas, if they go to the North, they have merely political freedom with no assurance of an opportunity in the economic world. But not a few of these have given themselves up to unrelenting toil with a view to accumulating sufficient wealth to move North and live thereafter on the income from their investments. Many of this class now spend some of their time in the North to educate their children. But they do not like to have these children who have been under refining influences return to the South to suffer the humiliation which during the last generation has been growing more and more aggravating. Endeavoring to carry out their policy of keeping the Negro down, southerners too often carefully plan to humiliate the progressive and intelligent blacks and in some cases form mobs to drive them out, as they are bad examples for that class of Negroes whom they desire to keep as menials.

There are also the migrating educated Negroes. They have studied history, law and economics and well understand what it is to get the rights guaranteed them by the constitution. The more they know the more discontented they become. They cannot speak out for what they want. No one is likely to second such a protest, not even the Negroes themselves, so generally have they been intimidated. The more outspoken they become, moreover, the more necessary is it for them to leave, for they thereby destroy their chances to earn a livelihood. White men in control of the public schools of the South see to it that the subserviency of the Negro teachers employed be certified beforehand. They dare not complain too much about equipment and salaries even if the per capita appropriation for the education of the Negroes be one fourth of that for the whites.

In the higher institutions of learning, especially the State schools, it is exceptional to find a principal who has the confidence of the Negroes. The Negroes will openly assert that he is in the pay of the reactionary whites, whose purpose is to keep the Negro down; and the incumbent himself will tell his board of regents how much he is opposed by the Negroes because he labors for the interests of the white race. Out of such sycophancy it is easily explained why our State schools have been so ineffective as to necessitate the sending of the Negro youth to private institutions maintained by northern philanthropy. Yet if an outspoken Negro happens to be an instructor in a private school conducted by educators from the North, he has to be careful about contending for a square deal; for, if the head of his institution does not suggest to him to proceed conservatively, the mob will dispose of the complainant. Physicians, lawyers and preachers, who are not so economically dependent as teachers can exercise no more freedom of speech in the midst of this triumphant rule of the lawless.

A large number of educated Negroes, therefore, have on account of these conditions been compelled to leave the South. Finding in the North, however, practically nothing in their line to do, because of the proscription by race prejudice and trades unions, many of them lead the life of menials, serving as waiters, porters, butlers and chauffeurs. While in Chicago, not long ago, the writer was in the office of a graduate of a colored southern college, who was showing his former teacher the picture of his class. In accounting for his classmates in the various walks of life, he reported that more than one third of them were settled to the occupation of Pullman porters.

The largest number of Negroes who have gone North during this period, however, belong to the intelligent laboring class. Some of them have become discontented for the very same reasons that the higher classes have tired of oppression in the South, but the larger number of them have gone North to improve their economic condition. Most of these have migrated to the large cities in the East and Northwest, such as Philadelphia, New York, Indianapolis, Pittsburgh, Cleveland, Columbus, Detroit and Chicago. To understand this problem in its urban aspects the accompanying diagram showing the increase in the Negro population of northern cities during the first decade of this century will be helpful.

Some of these Negroes have migrated after careful consideration; others have just happened to go north as wanderers; and a still larger number on the many excursions to the cities conducted by railroads during the summer months. Sometimes one excursion brings to Chicago two or three thousand Negroes, two thirds of whom never go back. They do not often follow the higher pursuits of labor in the North but they earn more money than they have been accustomed to earn in the South. They are attracted also by the liberal attitude of some whites, which, although not that of social equality, gives the Negroes a liberty in northern centers which leads them to think that they are citizens of the country.

This shifting in the population has had an unusually significant effect on the black belt. Frederick Douglass advised the Negroes in 1879 to remain in the South where they would be in sufficiently large numbers to have political power, but they have gradually scattered from the black belt so as to diminish greatly their chances ever to become the political force they formerly were in this country. The Negroes once had this possibility in South Carolina, Georgia, Alabama, Mississippi and Louisiana and, had the process of Africanization prior to the Civil War had a few decades longer to do its work, there would not have been any doubt as to the ultimate preponderance of the Negroes in those commonwealths. The tendencies of the black population according to the censuses of the United States and especially that of 1910, however, show that the chances for the control of these State governments by Negroes no longer exist except in South Carolina and Mississippi. It has been predicted, therefore, that, if the same tendencies continue for the next fifty years, there will be even few counties in which the Negroes will be in a majority. All of the Southern States except

Arkansas showed a proportionate increase of the white population over that of the black between 1900 and 1910, while West Virginia and Oklahoma with relatively small numbers of blacks showed, for reasons stated elsewhere, an increase in the Negro population. Thus we see coming to pass something like the proposed plan of Jefferson and other statesmen who a hundred years ago advocated the expansion of slavery to lessen the evil of the institution by distributing its burdens.

The migration of intelligent blacks, however, has been attended with several handicaps to the race. The large part of the black population is in the South and there it will stay for decades to come. The southern Negroes, therefore, have been robbed of their due part of the talented tenth. The educated blacks have had no constituency in the North and, consequently, have been unable to realize their sweetest dreams of the land of the free. In their new home the enlightened Negro must live with his light under a bushel. Those left behind in the South soon despair of seeing a brighter day and yield to the yoke. In the places of the leaders who were wont to speak for their people, the whites have raised up Negroes who accept favors offered them on the condition that their lips be sealed up forever on the rights of the Negro.

This emigration too has left the Negro subject to other evils. There are many first-class Negro business men in the South, but although there were once progressive men of color, who endeavored to protect the blacks from being plundered by white sharks and harpies there have arisen numerous unscrupulous Negroes who have for a part of the proceeds from such jobbery associated themselves with ill-designing white men to dupe illiterate Negroes. This trickery is brought into play in marketing their crops, selling them supplies, or purchasing their property. To carry out this iniquitous plan the persons concerned have the protection of the law, for while Negroes in general are imposed upon, those engaged in robbing them have no cause to fear.

CHAPTER 9. THE EXODUS DURING THE WORLD WAR

Within the last two years there has been a steady stream of Negroes into the North in such large numbers as to overshadow in its results all other movements of the kind in the United States. These Negroes have come largely from Alabama, Tennessee, Florida, Georgia, Virginia, North Carolina, Kentucky, South Carolina, Arkansas and Mississippi. The given causes of this migration are numerous and complicated. Some untruths centering around this exodus have not been unlike those of other migrations. Again we hear that the Negroes are being brought North to fight organized labor, and to carry doubtful States for the Republicans. These numerous explanations themselves, however, give rise to doubt as to the fundamental cause.

Why then should the Negroes leave the South? It has often been spoken of as the best place for them. There, it is said, they have made unusual strides forward. The progress of the Negroes in the South, however, has in no sense been general, although the land owned by Negroes in the country and the property of thrifty persons of their race in urban communities may be extensive. In most parts of the South the Negroes are still unable to become landowners or successful business men. Conditions and customs have reserved these spheres for the whites. Generally speaking, the Negroes are still dependent on the white people for food and shelter. Although not exactly slaves, they are yet attached to the white people as tenants, servants or dependents. Accepting this as their lot, they have been content to wear their lord's cast-off clothing, and live in his ramshackled barn or cellar. In this unhappy state so many have settled down, losing all ambition to attain a higher station. The world has gone on but in their sequestered sphere progress has passed them by.

What then is the cause? There have been bulldozing, terrorism, maltreatment and what not of persecution; but the Negroes have not in large numbers wandered away from the land of their birth. What the migrants themselves think about it, goes to the very heart of the trouble. Some say that they left the South on account of injustice in the courts, unrest, lack of privileges, denial of the right to vote, bad treatment, oppression, segregation or lynching. Others say that they left to find employment, to secure better wages, better school facilities, and better opportunities to toil upward. Southern white newspapers unaccustomed to give the Negroes any mention but that of criminals have said that the Negroes are going North because they have not had a fair chance in the South and that if they are to be retained there, the attitude of the whites toward them must be changed. Professor William O. Scroggs, of Louisiana State University, considers as causes of this exodus "the relatively low wages paid farm labor, an unsatisfactory tenant or crop-sharing system, the boll weevil, the crop failure of 1916, lynching, disfranchisement, segregation, poor schools, and the monotony, isolation and drudgery of farm life." Professor Scroggs, however, is wrong in thinking that the persecution of the blacks has little to do with the migration for the reason that during these years when the treatment of the Negroes is decidedly better they are leaving the South. This does not mean that they would not have left before, if they had had economic opportunities in the North. It is highly probable that the Negroes would not be leaving the South today, if they were treated as men, although there might be numerous opportunities for economic improvement in the North.

The immediate cause of this movement was the suffering due to the floods aggravated by the depredations of the boll weevil. Although generally mindful of our welfare, the United States Government has not been as ready to build levees against a natural enemy to property as it has been to provide fortifications for warfare. It has been necessary for local communities and State governments to tax themselves to maintain them. The national government, however, has appropriated to the purpose of facilitating inland navigation certain sums which have been used in doing this work, especially in the Mississippi Valley. There are now 1,538 miles of levees on both sides of the Mississippi from Cape Girardeau to the passes. These levees, of course, are still inadequate to the security of the planters against these inundations. Carrying 406 million tons of mud a year, the river becomes a dangerous stream subject to change, abandoning its old bed to cut for itself a new channel, transferring property from one State to another, isolating cities and leaving once useful levees marooned in the landscape like old Indian mounds or overgrown intrenchments.

This valley has, therefore, been frequently visited with disasters which have often set the population in motion. The first disastrous floods came in 1858 and 1859, breaking many of the levees, the destruction of which was practically completed by the floods of 1865 and 1869. There is an annual rise in the stream, but since 1874 this river system has fourteen times devastated large areas of this section with destructive floods. The property in this district depreciated in value to the extent of about 400 millions in ten years. Farmers from this section, therefore, have at times moved west with foreigners to take up public lands.

The other disturbing factor in this situation was the boll weevil, an interloper from Mexico in 1892. The boll weevil is an insect about one fourth of an inch in length, varying from one eighth to one third of an inch with a breadth of about one third of the length. When it first emerges it is yellowish, then becomes grayish brown and finally assumes a black shade. It breeds on no other plant than cotton and feeds on the boll. This little animal, at first attacked the cotton crop in Texas. It was not thought that it would extend its work into the heart of the South so as to become of national consequence, but it has, at the rate of forty to one hundred sixty miles annually, invaded all of the cotton district except that of the Carolinas and Virginia. The damage it does, varies according to the rainfall and the harshness of the winter, increasing with the former and decreasing with the latter. At times the damage has been to the extent of a loss of 50 per cent. of the crop, estimated at 400,000 bales of cotton annually, about 4,500,000 bales since the invasion or $250,000,000 worth of cotton. The output of the South being thus cut off, the planter has less income to provide supplies for his black tenants and, the prospects for future production being dark, merchants accustomed to give them credit have to refuse. This, of course, means financial depression, for the South is a borrowing section and any limitation to credit there blocks the wheels of industry. It was fortunate for the Negro laborers in this district that there was then a demand for labor in the North when this condition began to obtain.

This demand was made possible by the cutting off of European immigration by the World War, which thereby rendered this hitherto uncongenial section an inviting field for the Negro. The Negroes have made some progress in the North during the last fifty years, but despite their achievements they have been so handicapped by race prejudice and proscribed by trades unions that the uplift of the race by economic methods has been impossible. The European immigrants have hitherto excluded the Negroes even from the menial positions. In the midst of the drudgery left for them, the blacks have often heretofore been debased to the status of dependents and paupers.

Scattered through the North too in such small numbers, they have been unable to unite for social betterment and mutual improvement and naturally too weak to force the community to respect their wishes as could be done by a large group with some political or economic power. At present, however, Negro laborers, who once went from city to city, seeking such employment as trades unions left to them, can work even as skilled laborers throughout the North. Women of color formerly excluded from domestic service by foreign maids are now in demand. Many mills and factories which Negroes were prohibited from entering a few years ago are now bidding for their labor. Railroads cannot find help to keep their property in repair, contractors fall short of their plans for failure to hold mechanics drawn into the industrial boom and the United States Government has had to advertise for men to hasten the preparation for war.

Men from afar went south to tell the Negroes of a way of escape to a more congenial place. Blacks long since unaccustomed to venture a few miles from home, at once had visions of a promised land just a few hundred miles away. Some were told of the chance to amass fabulous riches, some of the opportunities for education and some of the hospitality of the places of amusement and recreation in the North. The migrants then were soon on the way. Railway stations became conspicuous with the presence of Negro tourists, the trains were crowded to full capacity and the streets of northern cities were soon congested with black laborers seeking to realize their dreams in the land of unusual opportunity.

Employment agencies, recently multiplied to meet the demand for labor, find themselves unable to cope with the situation and agents sent into the South to induce the blacks by offers of free transportation and high wages to go north, have found it impossible to supply the demand in centers where once toiled the Poles, Italians and the Greeks formerly preferred to the Negroes. In other words, the present migration differs from others in that the Negro has opportunity awaiting him in the North whereas formerly it was necessary for him to make a place for himself upon arriving among enemies. The proportion of those returning to the South, therefore, will be inconsiderable.

Becoming alarmed at the immensity of this movement the South has undertaken to check it. To frighten Negroes from the North southern newspapers are carefully circulating reports that many of them are returning to their native land because of unexpected hardships. But having failed in this, southerners have compelled employment agents to cease operations there, arrested suspected employers and, to prevent the departure of the Negroes, imprisoned on false charges those who appear at stations to leave for the North. This procedure could not long be effective, for by the more legal and clandestine methods of railway passenger agents the work has gone forward. Some southern communities have, therefore, advocated drastic legislation against labor agents, as was suggested in Louisiana in 1914, when by operation of the Underwood Tariff Law the Negroes thrown out of employment in the sugar district migrated to the cotton plantations.

One should not, however, get the impression that the majority of the Negroes are leaving the South. Eager as these Negroes seem to go, there is no unanimity of opinion as to whether migration is the best policy. The sycophant, toady class of Negroes naturally advise the blacks to remain in the South to serve their white neighbors. The radical protagonists of the equal-rights-for-all element urge them to come North by all means. Then there are the thinking Negroes, who are still further divided. Both divisions of this element have the interests of the race at heart, but they are unable to agree as to exactly what the blacks should now do. Thinking that the present war will soon be over and that consequently the immigration of foreigners into this country will again set in and force out of employment thousands of Negroes who have migrated to the North, some of the most representative Negroes are advising their fellows to remain where they are. The most serious objection to this transplantation is that it means for the Negroes a loss of land, the rapid acquisition of which has long been pointed to as the best evidence of the ability of the blacks to rise in the economic world. So many Negroes who have by dint of energy purchased small farms yielding an increasing income from year to year, are now disposing of them at nominal prices to come north to work for wages. Looking beyond the war, however, and thinking too that the depopulation of Europe during this upheaval will render immigration from that quarter for some years an impossibility, other thinkers urge the Negroes to continue the migration to the North, where the race may be found in sufficiently large numbers to wield economic and political power.

Great as is the dearth of labor in the South, moreover, the Negro exodus has not as yet caused such a depression as to unite the whites in inducing the blacks to remain in that section. In the first place, the South has not yet felt the worst effects of this economic upheaval as that part of the country has been unusually aided by the millions which the United States Government is daily spending there. Furthermore, the poor whites are anxious to see the exodus of their competitors in the field of labor. This leaves the capitalists at their mercy, and in keeping with their domineering attitude, they will be able to handle the labor situation as they desire. As an evidence of this fact we need but note the continuation of mob rule and lynching in the South despite the preachings against it of the organs of thought which heretofore winked at it. This terrorism has gone to an unexpected extent. Negro farmers have been threatened with bodily injury, unless they leave certain parts.

The southerner of aristocratic bearing will say that only the shiftless poor whites terrorize the Negroes. This may be so, but the truth offers little consolation when we observe that most white people in the South are of this class; and the tendency of this element to put their children to work before they secure much education does not indicate that the South will soon experience that general enlightenment necessary to exterminate these survivals of barbarism. Unless the upper classes of the whites can bring the mob around to their way of thinking that the persecution of the Negro is prejudicial to the interests of all, it is not likely that mob rule will soon cease and the migration to this extent will be promoted rather than retarded.

It is unfortunate for the South that the growing consciousness of the Negroes has culminated at the very time they are most needed. Finally heeding the advice of agricultural experts to reconstruct its agricultural system, the South has learned in the school of bitter experience to depart from the plan of producing the single cotton crop. It is now raising food-stuffs to make that section self-supporting without reducing the usual output of cotton. With the increasing production in the South, therefore, more labor is needed just at the very time it is being drawn to centers in the North. The North being an industrial and commercial section has usually attracted the immigrants, who will never fit into the economic situation in the South because they will not accept the treatment given Negroes. The South, therefore, is now losing the only labor which it can ever use under present conditions.

Where these Negroes are going is still more interesting. The exodus to the west was mainly directed to Kansas and neighboring States, the migration to the Southwest centered in Oklahoma and Texas, pioneering Negro laborers drifted into the industrial district of the Appalachian highland during the eighties and nineties and the infiltration of the discontented talented tenth affected largely the cities of the North. But now we are told that at the very time the mining districts of the North and West are being filled with blacks the western planters are supplying their farms with them and that into some cities have gone sufficient skilled and unskilled Negro workers to increase the black population more than one hundred per cent. Places in the North, where the black population has not only not increased but even decreased in recent years, are now receiving a steady influx of Negroes. In fact, this is a nation-wide migration affecting all parts and all conditions.

Students of social problems are now wondering whether the Negro can be adjusted in the North. Many perplexing problems must arise. This movement will produce results not unlike those already mentioned in the discussion of other migrations, some of which we have evidence of today.

There will be an increase in race prejudice leading in some communities to actual outbreaks as in Chester and Youngstown and probably to massacres like that of East St. Louis, in which participated not only well-known citizens but the local officers and the State militia. The Negroes in the North are in competition with white men who consider them not only strike breakers but a sort of inferior individuals unworthy of the consideration which white men deserve. And this condition obtains even where Negroes have been admitted to the trades unions.

Negroes in seeking new homes in the North, moreover, invade residential districts hitherto exclusively white. There they encounter prejudice and persecution until most whites thus disturbed move out determined to do whatever they can to prevent their race from suffering from further depreciation of property and the disturbance of their community life.

Lawlessness has followed, showing that violence may under certain conditions develop among some classes anywhere rather than reserve itself for vigilance committees of primitive communities. It has brought out too another aspect of lawlessness in that it breaks out in the North where the numbers of Negroes are still too small to serve as an excuse for the terrorism and lynching considered necessary in the South to keep the Negroes down.

The maltreatment of the Negroes will be nationalized by this exodus. The poor whites of both sections will strike at this race long stigmatized by servitude but now demanding economic equality. Race prejudice, the fatal weakness of the Americans, will not so soon abate although there will be advocates of fraternity, equality and liberty required to reconstruct our government and rebuild our civilization in conformity with the demands of modern efficiency by placing every man regardless of his color wherever he may do the greatest good for the greatest number.

The Negroes, however, are doubtless going to the North in sufficiently large numbers to make themselves felt. If this migration falls short of establishing in that section Negro colonies large enough to wield economic and political power, their state in the end will not be any better than that of the Negroes already there. It is to these large numbers alone that we must look for an agent to counteract the development of race feeling into riots. In large numbers the blacks will be able to strike for better wages or concessions due a rising laboring class and they will have enough votes to defeat for reelection those officers who wink at mob violence or treat Negroes as persons beyond the pale of the law.

The Negroes in the North, however, will get little out of the harvest if, like the blacks of Reconstruction days, they unwisely concentrate their efforts on solving all of their problems by electing men of their race as local officers or by sending a few members even to Congress as is likely in New York, Philadelphia and Chicago within the next generation. The Negroes have had representatives in Congress before but they were put out because their constituency was uneconomic and politically impossible. There was nothing but the mere letter of the law behind the Reconstruction Negro officeholder and the thus forced political recognition against public opinion could not last any longer than natural forces for some time thrown out of gear by unnatural causes could resume the usual line of procedure.

It would be of no advantage to the Negro race today to send to Congress forty Negro Representatives on the pro rata basis of numbers, especially if they happened not to be exceptionally well qualified. They would remain in Congress only so long as the American white people could devise some plan for eliminating them as they did during the Reconstruction period. Near as the world has approached real democracy, history gives no record of a permanent government conducted on this basis. Interests have always been stronger than numbers. The Negroes in the North, therefore, should not on the eve of the economic revolution follow the advice of their misguided and misleading race leaders who are diverting their attention from their actual welfare to a specialization in politics. To concentrate their efforts on electing a few Negroes to office wherever the blacks are found in the majority, would exhibit the narrowness of their oppressors. It would be as unwise as the policy of the Republican party of setting aside a few insignificant positions like that of Recorder of Deeds, Register of the Treasury and Auditor of the Navy as segregated jobs for Negroes. Such positions have furnished a nucleus for the large, worthless, office-seeking class of Negroes in Washington, who have established the going of the people of the city toward pretence and sham.

The Negroes should support representative men of any

color or party, if they stand for a square deal and equal rights for all. The new Negroes in the North, therefore, will, as so many of their race in New York, Philadelphia and Chicago are now doing, ally themselves with those men who are fairminded and considerate of the man far down, and seek to embrace their many opportunities for economic progress, a foundation for political recognition, upon which the race must learn to build. Every race in the universe must aspire to becoming a factor in politics; but history shows that there is no short route to such success. Like other despised races beset with the prejudice and militant opposition of self-styled superiors, the Negroes must increase their industrial efficiency, improve their opportunities to make a living, develop the home, church and school, and contribute to art, literature, science and philosophy to clear the way to that political freedom of which they cannot be deprived.

The entire country will be benefited by this upheaval. It will be helpful even to the South. The decrease in the black population in those communities where the Negroes outnumber the whites will remove the fear of Negro domination, one of the causes of the backwardness of the South and its peculiar civilization. Many of the expensive precautions which the southern people have taken to keep the Negroes down, much of the terrorism incited to restrain the blacks from self-assertion will no longer be considered necessary; for, having the excess in numbers on their side, the whites will finally rest assured that the Negroes may be encouraged without any apprehension that they may develop enough power to subjugate or embarrass their former masters.

The Negroes too are very much in demand in the South and the intelligent whites will gladly give them larger opportunities to attach them to that section, knowing that the blacks, once conscious of their power to move freely throughout the country wherever they may improve their condition, will never endure hardships like those formerly inflicted upon the race. The South is already learning that the Negro is the most desirable laborer for that section, that the persecution of Negroes not only drives them out but makes the employment of labor such a problem that the South will not be an attractive section for capital. It will, therefore, be considered the duty of business men to secure protection to the Negroes lest their ill-treatment force them to migrate to the extent of bringing about a stagnation of their business.

The exodus has driven home the truth that the prosperity of the South is at the mercy of the Negro. Dependent on cheap labor, which the bulldozing whites will not readily furnish, the wealthy southerners must finally reach the position of regarding themselves and the Negroes as having a community of interests which each must promote. "Nature itself in those States," Douglass said, "came to the rescue of the Negro. He had labor, the South wanted it, and must have it or perish. Since he was free he could then give it, or withhold it; use it where he was, or take it elsewhere, as he pleased. His labor made him a slave and his labor could, if he would, make him free, comfortable and independent. It is more to him than either fire, sword, ballot boxes or bayonets. It touches the heart of the South through its pocket." Knowing that the Negro has this silent weapon to be used against his employer or the community, the South is already giving the race better educational facilities, better railway accommodations, and will eventually, if the advocacy of certain southern newspapers be heeded, grant them political privileges. Wages in the South, therefore, have risen even in the extreme southwestern States, where there is an opportunity to import Mexican labor. Reduced to this extremity, the southern aristocrats have begun to lose some of their race prejudice, which has not hitherto yielded to reason or philanthropy.

Southern men are telling their neighbors that their section

must abandon the policy of treating the Negroes as a problem and construct a program for recognition rather than for repression. Meetings are, therefore, being held to find out what the Negro wants and what may be done to keep them contented. They are told that the Negro must be elevated not exploited, that to make the South what it must needs be, the cooperation of all is needed to train and equip the men of all races for efficiency. The aim of all then must be to reform or get rid of the unfair proprietors who do not give their tenants a fair division of the returns from their labor. To this end the best whites and blacks are urged to come together to find a working basis for a systematic effort in the interest of all.

To say that either the North or the South can easily become adjusted to this change is entirely too sanguine. The North will have a problem. The Negroes in the northern city will have much more to contend with than when settled in the rural districts or small urban centers. Forced by restrictions of real estate men into congested districts, there has appeared the tendency toward further segregation. They are denied social contact, are sagaciously separated from the whites in public places of amusement and are clandestinely segregated in public schools in spite of the law to the contrary. As a consequence the Negro migrant often finds himself with less friends than he formerly had. The northern man who once denounced the South on account of its maltreatment of the blacks gradually grows silent when a Negro is brought next door. There comes with the movement, therefore, the difficult problem of housing.

Where then must the migrants go? They are not wanted by the whites and are treated with contempt by the native blacks of the northern cities, who consider their brethren from the South too criminal and too vicious to be tolerated. In the average progressive city there has heretofore been a certain increase in the number of houses through natural growth, but owing to the high cost of materials, high wages, increasing taxation and the inclination to invest money in enterprises growing out of the war, fewer houses are now being built, although Negroes are pouring into these centers as a steady stream. The usual Negro quarters in northern centers of this sort have been filled up and the overflow of the black population scattered throughout the city among white people. Old warehouses, store rooms, churches, railroad cars and tents have been used to meet these demands.

A large per cent of these Negroes are located in rooming houses or tenements for several families. The majority of them cannot find individual rooms. Many are crowded into the same room, therefore, and too many into the same bed. Sometimes as many as four and five sleep in one bed, and that may be placed in the basement, dining-room or kitchen where there is neither adequate light nor air. In some cases men who work during the night sleep by day in beds used by others during the night. Some of their houses have no water inside and have toilets on the outside without sewerage connections. The cooking is often done by coal or wood stoves or kerosene lamps. Yet the rent runs high although the houses are generally out of repair and in some cases have been condemned by the municipality. The unsanitary conditions in which many of the blacks are compelled to live are in violation of municipal ordinances.

Furthermore, because of the indiscriminate employment by labor agents and the dearth of labor requiring the acceptance of almost all sorts of men, some disorderly and worthless Negroes have been brought into the North. On the whole, however, these migrants are not lazy, shiftless and desperate as some predicted that they would be. They generally attend church, save their money and send a part of their savings regularly to their families. They do not belong to the class going North in quest of whiskey. Mr. Abraham Epstein, who has written a valuable pamphlet setting forth his researches in Pittsburgh, states that the migrants of that city do not generally imbibe and most of those who do, take beer only. Out of four hundred and seventy persons to whom he propounded this question, two hundred and ten or forty-four per cent of them were total abstainers. Seventy per cent of those having families do not drink at all.

With this congestion, however, have come serious difficulties. Crowded conditions give rise to vice, crime and disease. The prevalence of vice has not been the rule but tendencies, which better conditions in the South restrained from developing, have under these undesirable conditions been given an opportunity to grow. There is, therefore, a tendency toward the crowding of dives, assembling on the corners of streets and the commission of petty offences which crowd them into the police courts. One finds also sometimes a congestion in houses of dissipation and the carrying of concealed weapons. Law abiding on the whole, however, they have not experienced a wave of crime. The chief offences are those resulting from the saloons and denizens of vice, which are furnished by the community itself.

Disease has been one of their worst enemies, but reports on their health have been exaggerated. On account of this sudden change of the Negroes from one climate to another and the hardships of more unrelenting toil, many of them have been unable to resist pneumonia, bronchitis and tuberculosis. Churches, rescue missions and the National League on Urban Conditions Among Negroes have offered relief in some of these cases. The last-named organization is serving in large cities as a sort of clearing house for such activities and as means of interpreting one race to the other. It has now eighteen branches in cities to which this migration has been directed. Through a local worker these migrants are approached, properly placed and supervised until they can adjust themselves to the community without apparent embarrassment to either race. The League has been able to handle the migrants arriving by extending the work so as to know their movements beforehand.

The occupations in which these people engage will throw further light on their situation. About ninety per cent of them do unskilled labor. Only ten per cent of them do semi-skilled or skilled labor. They serve as common laborers, puddlers, mold-setters, painters, carpenters, bricklayers, cement workers and machinists. What the Negroes need then is that sort of freedom which carries with it industrial opportunity and social justice. This they cannot attain until they be permitted to enter the higher pursuits of labor. Two reasons are given for failure to enter these: first, that Negro labor is unstable and inefficient; and second, that white men will protest. Organized labor, however, has done nothing to help the blacks. Yet it is a fact that accustomed to the easy-going toil of the plantation, the blacks have not shown the same efficiency as that of the whites. Some employers report, however, that they are glad to have them because they are more individualistic and do not like to group. But it is not true that colored labor cannot be organized. The blacks have merely been neglected by organized labor. Wherever they have had the opportunity to do so, they have organized and stood for their rights like men. The trouble is that the trades unions are generally antagonistic to Negroes although they are now accepting the blacks in self-defense. The policy of excluding Negroes from these bodies is made effective by an evasive procedure, despite the fact that the constitutions of many of them specifically provide that there shall be no discrimination on account of race or color.

Because of this tendency some of the representatives of trades unions have asked why Negroes do not organize unions of their own. This the Negroes have generally failed to do, thinking that they would not be recognized by the American Federation of Labor, and knowing too that what their union would have to contend with in the economic world would be diametrically opposed to the wishes of the men from whom they would have to seek recognition. Organized labor, moreover, is opposed to the powerful capitalists, the only real friends the Negroes have in the North to furnish them food and shelter while their lives are often being sought by union members. Steps toward organizing Negro labor have been made in various Northern cities during 1917 and 1918. The objective of this movement for the present, however, is largely that of employment.

Eventually the Negro migrants will, no doubt, without much difficulty establish themselves among law-abiding and industrious people of the North where they will receive assistance. Many persons now see in this shifting of the Negro population the dawn of a new day, not in making the Negro numerically dominant anywhere to obtain political power, but to secure for him freedom of movement from section to section as a competitor in the industrial world. They also observe that while there may be an increase of race prejudice in the North the same will in that proportion decrease in the South, thus balancing the equation while giving the Negro his best chance in the economic world out of which he must emerge a real man with power to secure his rights as an American citizen.